VISUAL ELEMENTS 4

WORLD TRADITIONAL FOLK PATTERNS

VISUAL ELEMENTS 4

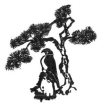 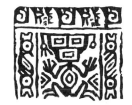 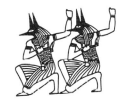

ROCKPORT PUBLISHERS • ROCKPORT, MASSACHUSETTS
Distributed by North Light Books • Cincinnati, Ohio

Distributed to the book trade and art trade in
the U.S. and Canada by:
North Light, an imprint of
Writer's Digest Books
1507 Dana Avenue
Cincinnati, Ohio 45207
(513) 985-0717

Other distribution by:
Rockport Publishers
5 Smith Street
Rockport, Massachusetts 01966
(617) 546-9590
Telex: 5106019284
Fax: (617) 546-7141

ISBN: 0-935603-12-3

First published in Japan. First English lan-
guage edition published by Rockport Publishers.

Visual Elements 4: World Folk Patterns was
produced by Blount & Company, Number
Twelve Station Road, Cranbury, New Jersey
08512, (609) 655-5785.

Printed in the United States.

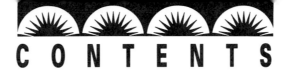

C O N T E N T S

Arab: Gold and silver ivory work	1	Syria: Decorative textile pattern	41	Europe: Buttercup flower pattern	81
Egypt: Sacred beetle, shallow cut relief	2	Medieval Europe: Diamond pattern	42	Europe: Rhododendron flower pattern	82
Egypt: Flowing decorative band, frieze	3	Lombardy: Bas-relief pattern	43	Europe: Acorn flower pattern	83
Egypt: Human figure pattern	4	Italy: Human figure pattern	44	India: Paisley pattern	84
Egypt: Lotus mixed with reed	5	Italy: Animal figure pattern	45	India: Plant figure pattern	85
Turkey: Flower and leaf design	6	Medieval Europe: Oriental-style pattern	46	India: Flower, bird and plant pattern	86
Persia: Ceramic pattern	7	Italy: Decorative pattern	47	India: Elephant and lotus flower	87
Persia: Bird and plant figure	8	Renaissance Europe: Human figure pattern	48	India: Elephant and horse pattern	88
Persia: Paisley pattern	9	Renaissance Europe: Vase design pattern	49	Borneo: Decorative pattern	89
Persia: Birds and roses	10	Renaissance Europe: Keyhole pattern	50	Java: Decorative pattern	90
Persia: Repeating pattern	11	France: Ceramic pattern	51	Java: Decorative pattern	91
Persia: Repeating pattern	12	France: Oriental-style pattern	52	Java: Decorative pattern	92
Greece: Stephany pattern	13	France: Animal figure pattern	53	China: Decorative pattern	93
Greece: Repeating pattern	14	France: Decorative pattern	54	China: Chinese phoenix pattern	94
Greece: Terra cotta pattern	15	Europe: Heraldic crest pattern	55	China: Flower and bird pattern	95
Greece: Palmette band pattern	16	France: Wall pattern	56	China: Sacred horse pattern	96
Byzantine: Pattern on circular window	17	Contemporary Europe: Repeating pattern	57	China: Dragon pattern	97
Greece: Syrian textile pattern	18	Italy: Repeating pattern	58	China: Dragon pattern	98
Greece: Terra cotta pattern	19	Roman Byzantine: Marble mosaic pattern	59	China: Flower and Chinese phoenix pattern	99
Greece: Animal and plant figures	20	Medieval Rome: Mosaic pattern	60	China: Confucius	100
Islamic: Repeating pattern	21	Roman Byzantine: Mosaic pattern	61	China: Decorative pattern	101
Islamic: Repeating pattern	22	Europe: Medieval-style driftwood pattern	62	China: Cloud and crystal drawn as wave	102
Islamic: Repeating pattern	23	England: Repeating pattern	63	Korea: Decorative pattern	103
Islamic: Repeating pattern	24	England: Animal figure pattern	64	Korea: Decorative pattern	104
Islamic: Repeating pattern	25	Ireland: Quilt decoration	65	Korea: Dragon print	105
Islamic: Repeating pattern	26	Ireland: Quilt decoration	66	Korea: Flower and fish pattern	106
Islamic: Repeating pattern	27	Europe: Medieval-style quilt decoration	67	Korea: Flower pattern	107
Islamic: Repeating pattern	28	Czechoslovakia: Repeating pattern	68	Korea: Animal figure pattern	108
Islamic: Repeating pattern	29	Russia: Gold sculpture work	69	Peru: Tool decoration	109
Islamic: Repeating pattern	30	Europe: Plant and flower pattern	70	Inca: Puma and bird pattern	110
Islamic: Repeating pattern	31	Europe: Iris flower pattern	71	Inca: Abstract fish pattern	111
Islamic: Repeating pattern	32	Europe: Water lily flower pattern	72	Inca: Animal face pattern	112
Islamic: Repeating pattern	33	Europe: Decorative flower pattern	73	Mexico: Human figure pattern	113
Islamic: Repeating pattern	34	Europe: Wisteria flower pattern	74	Mexico: Manuscript drawing	114
Islamic: Repeating pattern	35	Europe: Rose flower pattern	75	Native American: Human figure pattern	115
Islamic: Repeating pattern	36	Europe: Mallow flower pattern	76	Native American: Repeating pattern	116
Islamic: Repeating pattern	37	Europe: Decorative flower pattern	77	Native American: Human figure pattern	117
Islamic: Plant figure pattern	38	Europe: Decorative flower pattern	78	Native American: Lizard pattern	118
Islamic: Plant figure pattern	39	Europe: Iris flower pattern	79	United States: Heraldic pattern with cattle	119
Islamic: Plant figure pattern	40	Europe: Gourd pattern	80	Native American: Bird pattern	120

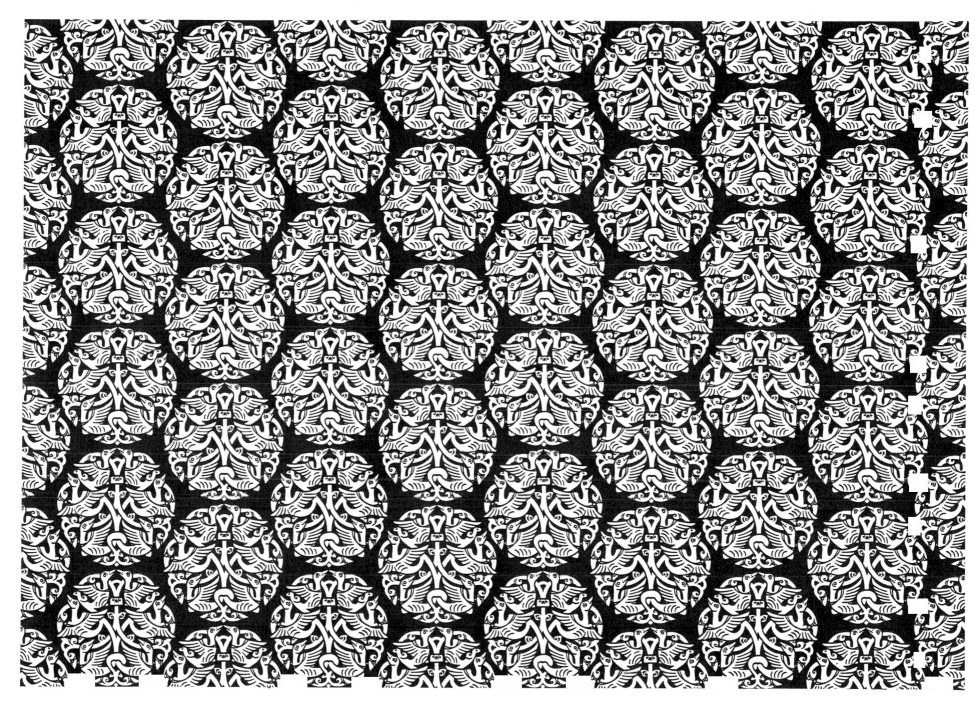

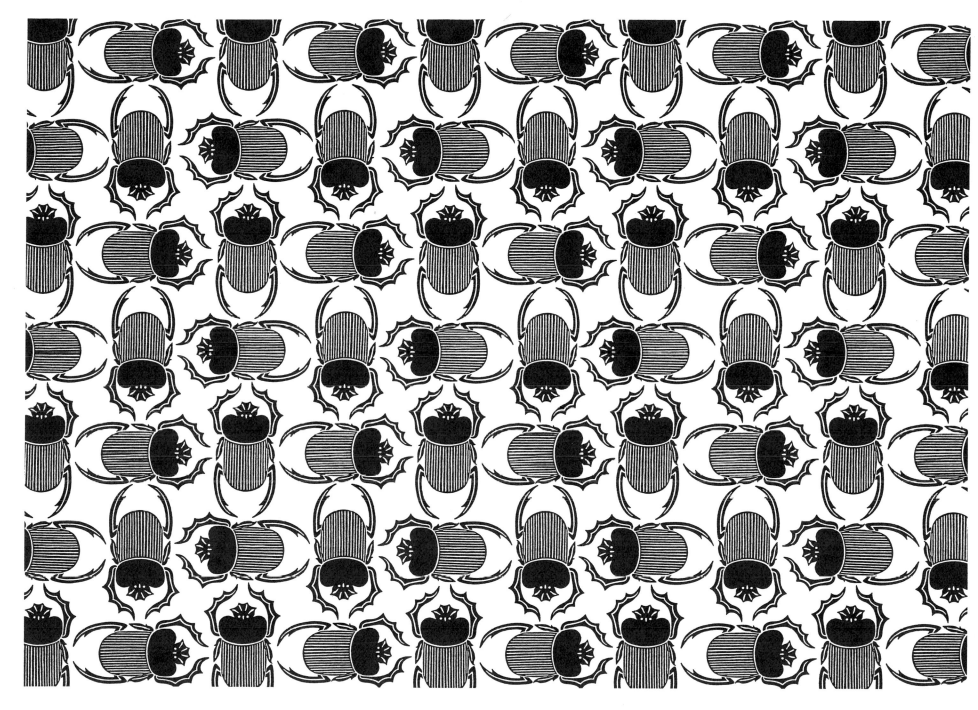

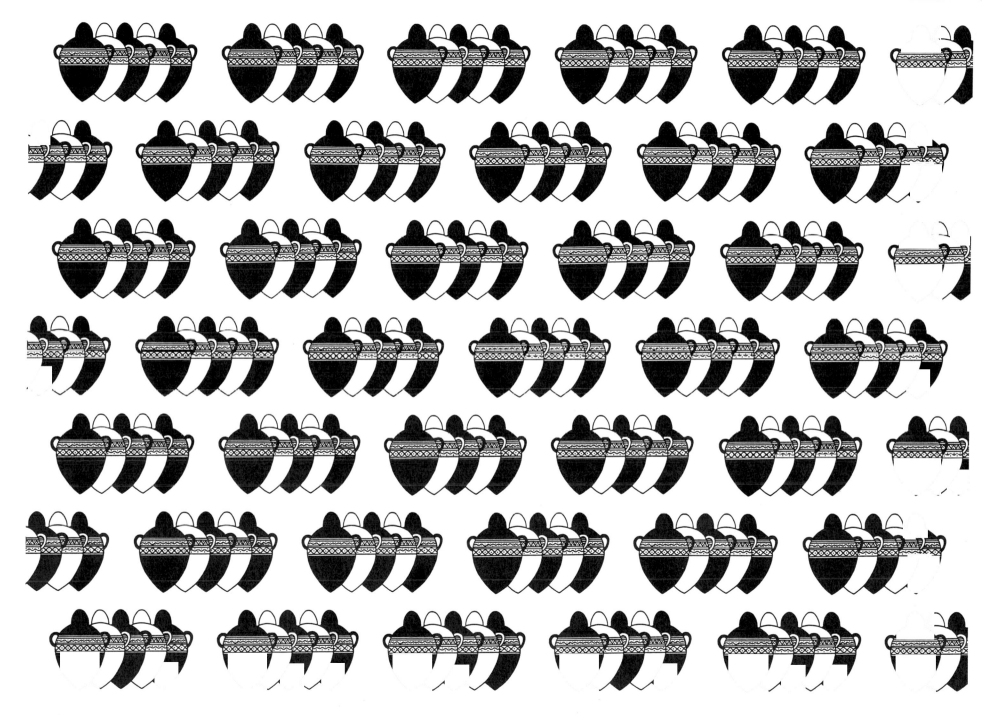

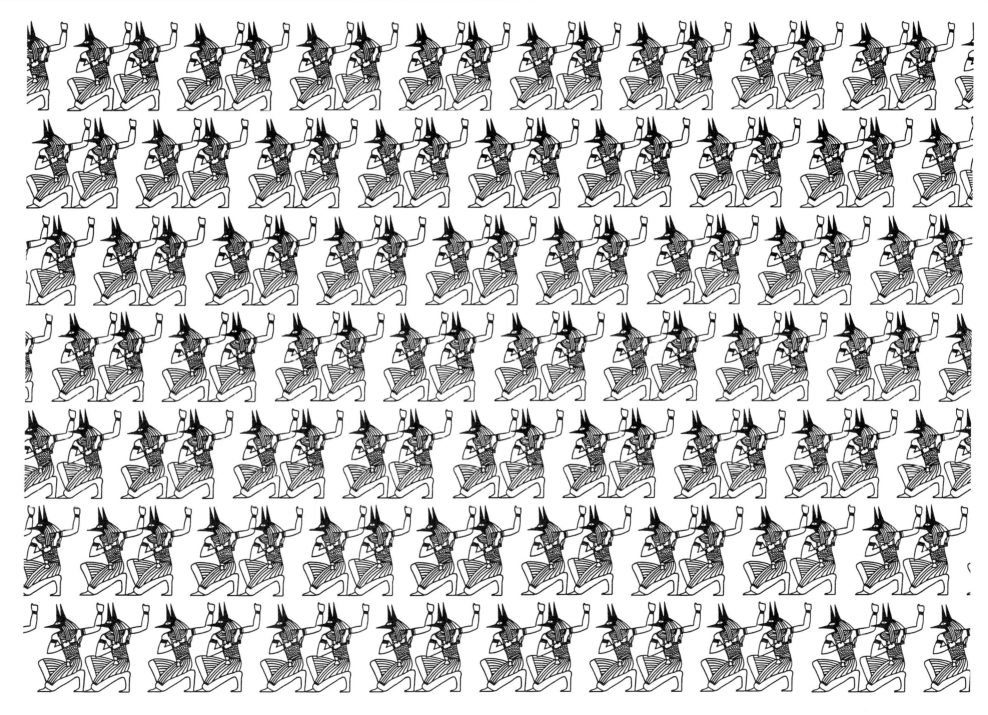

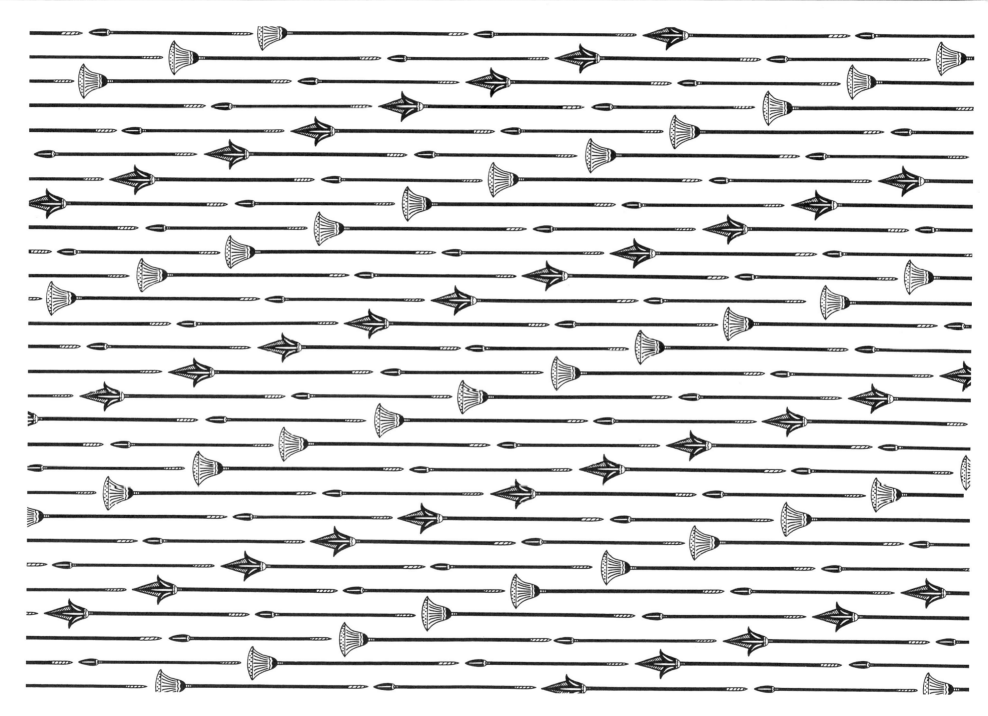

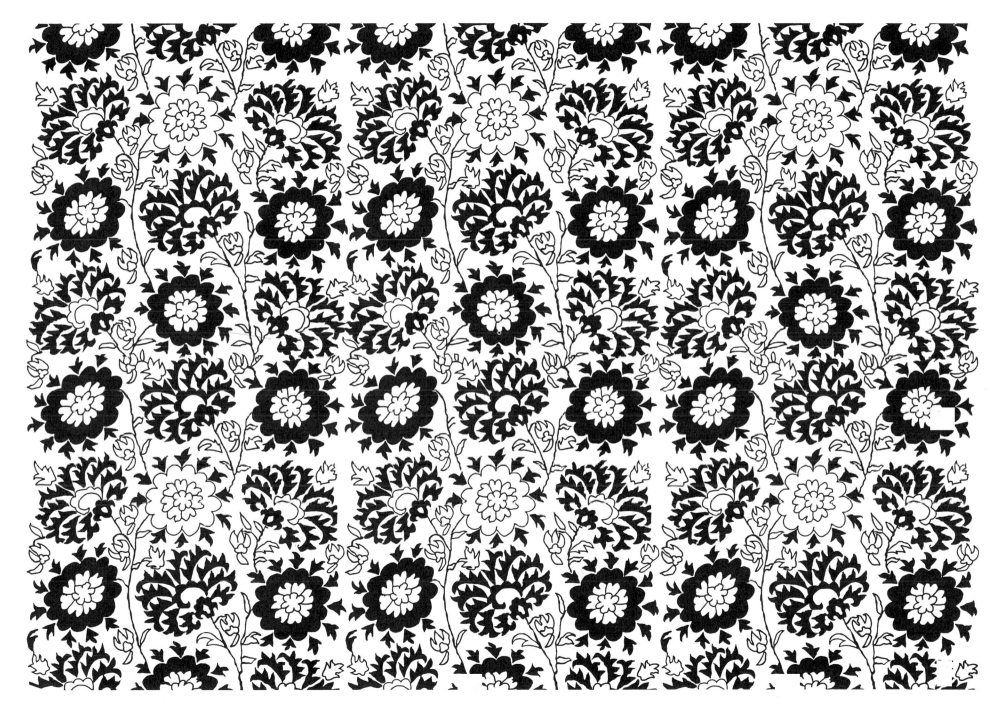

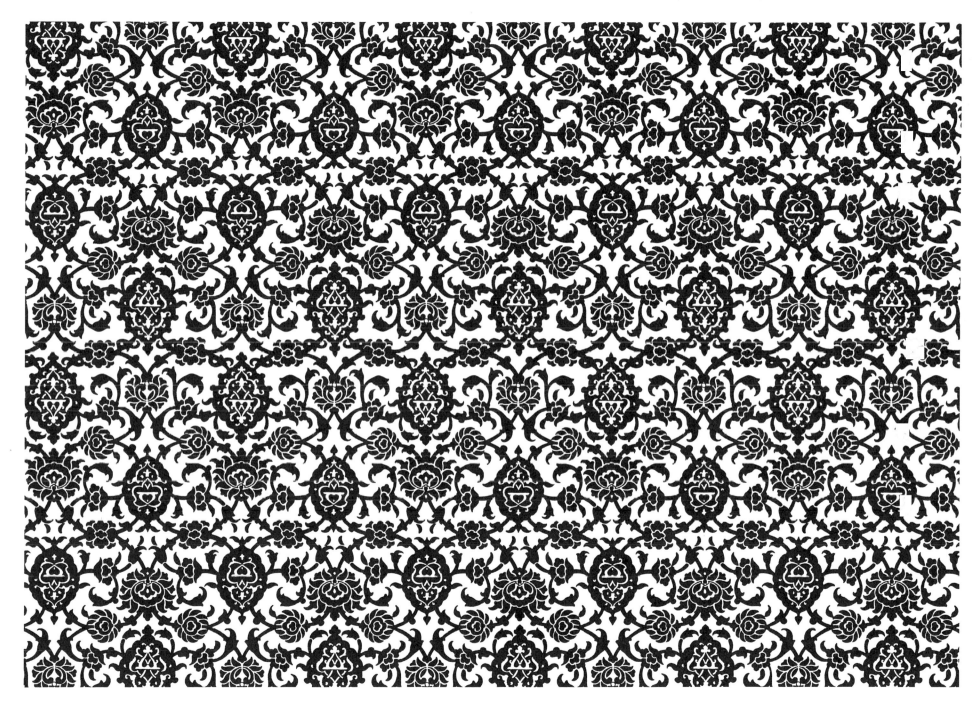

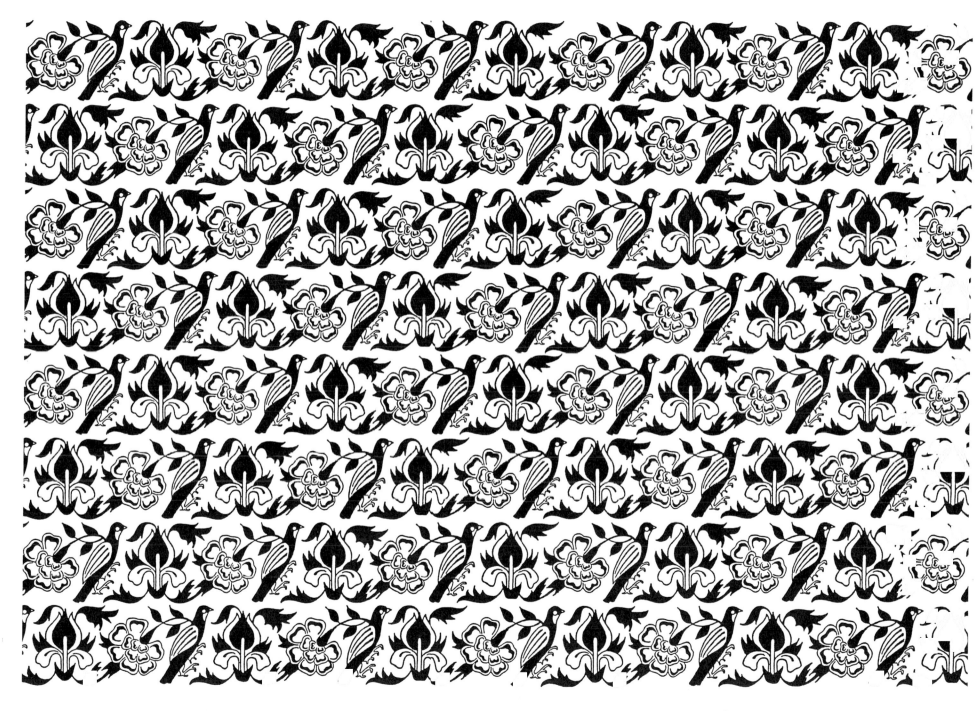

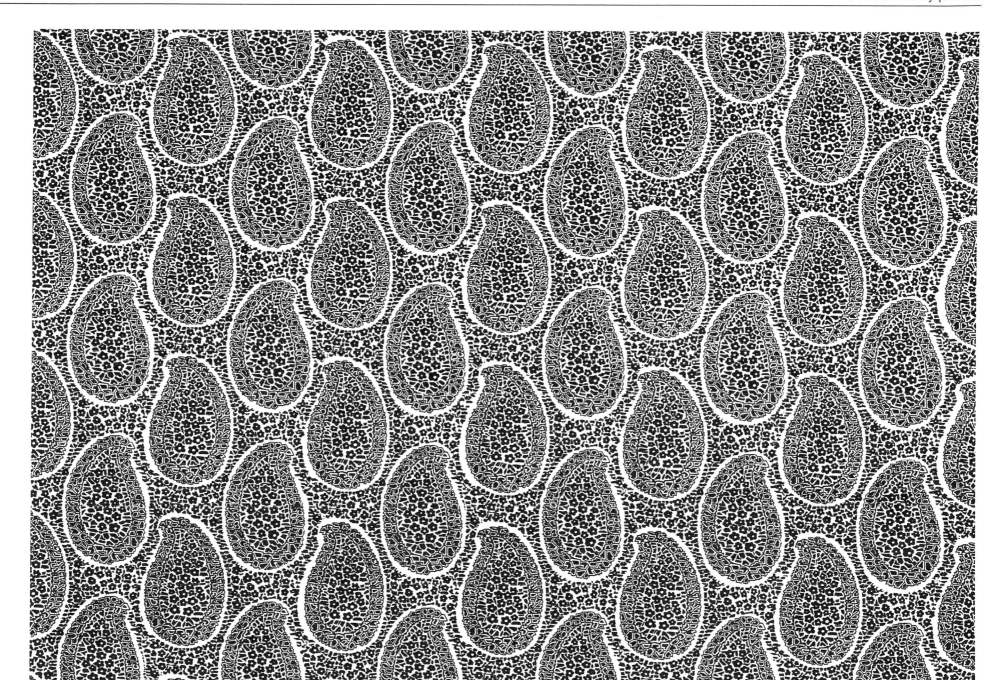

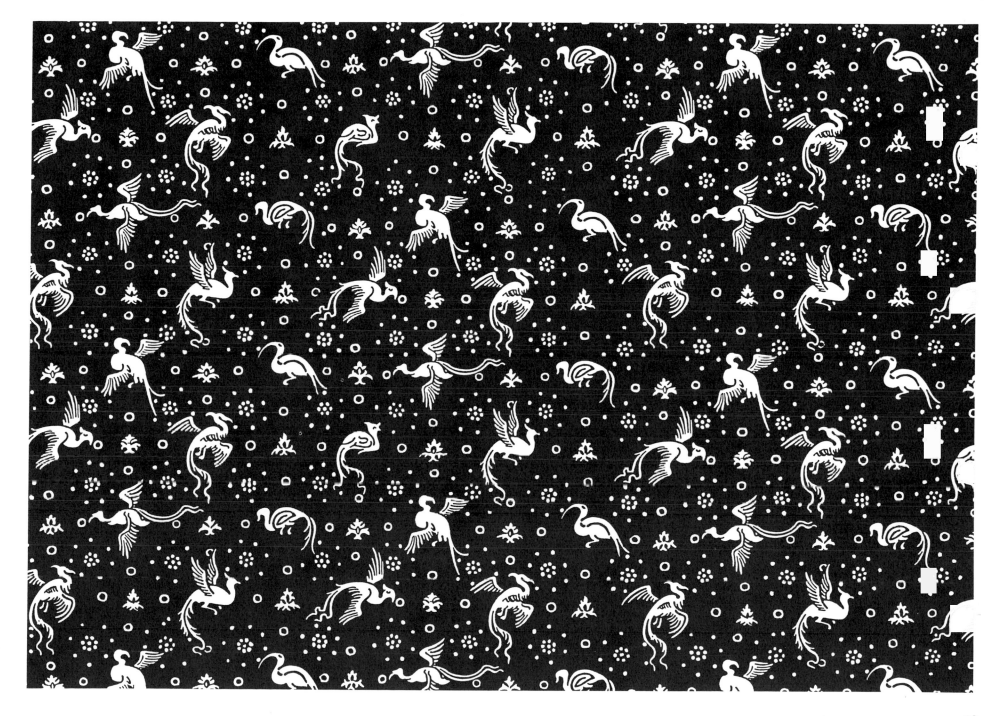

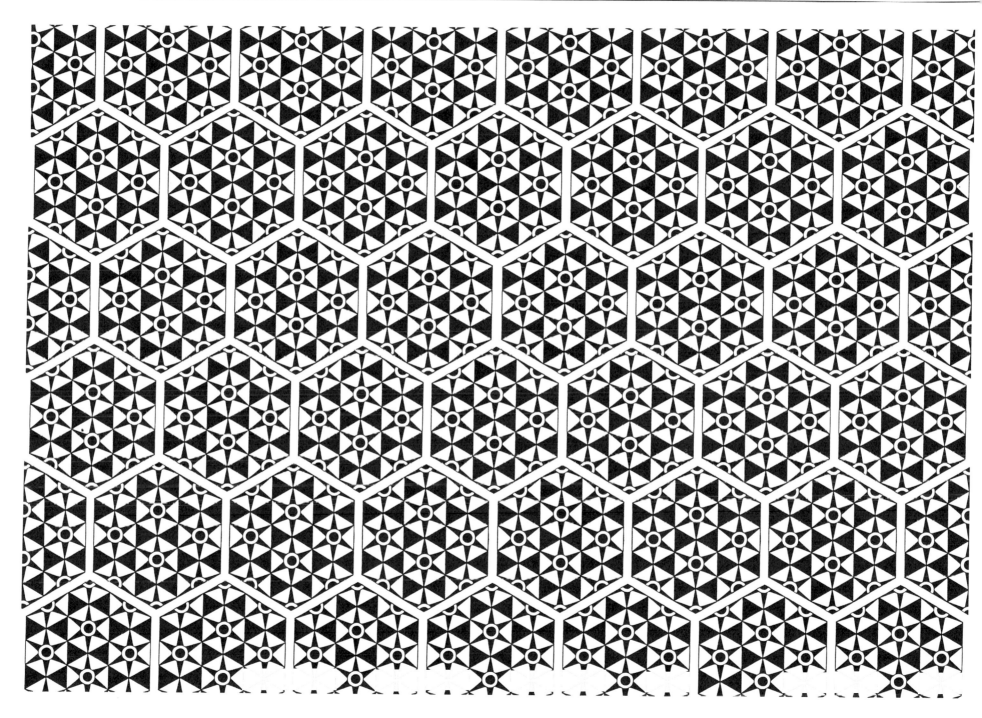

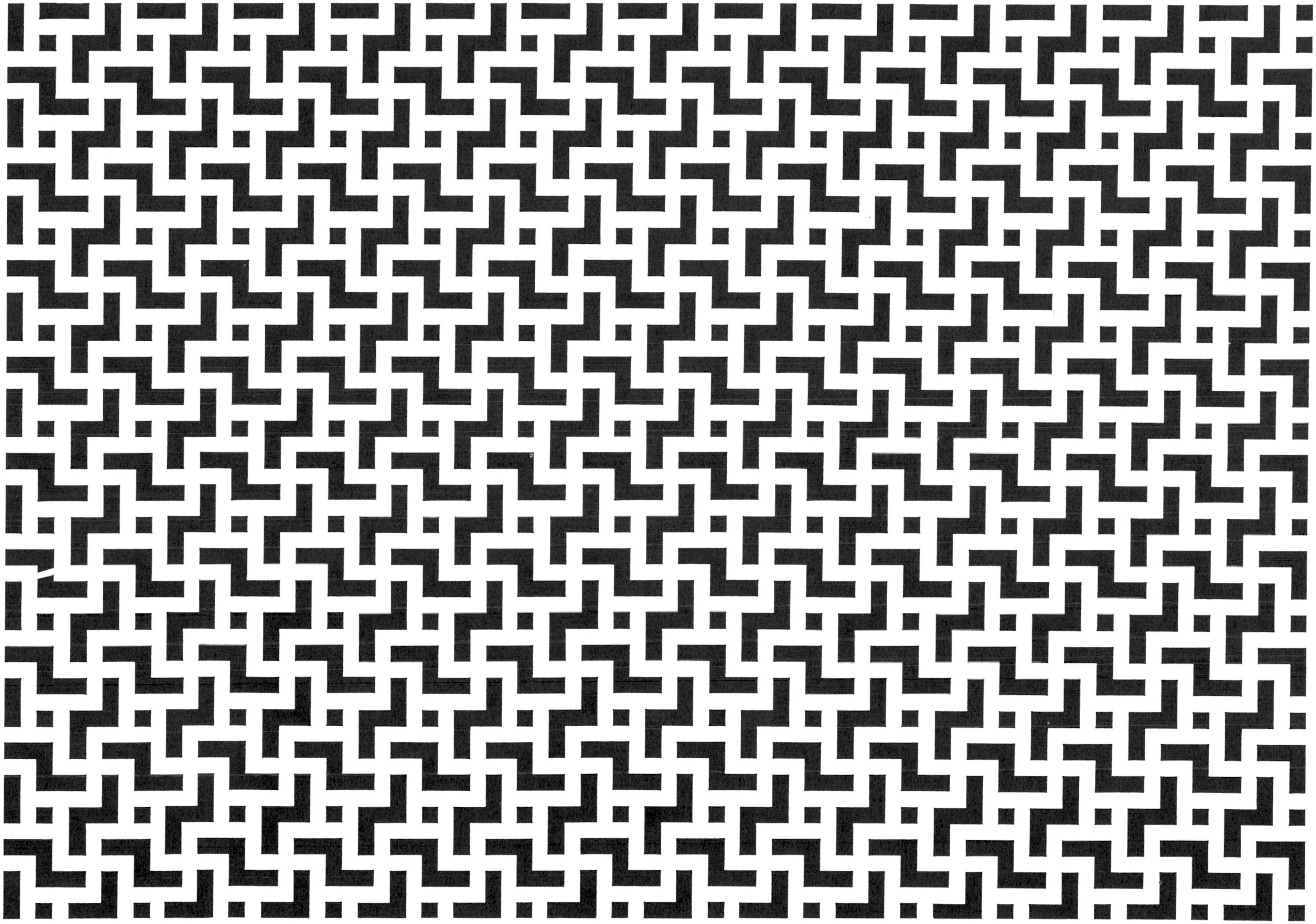

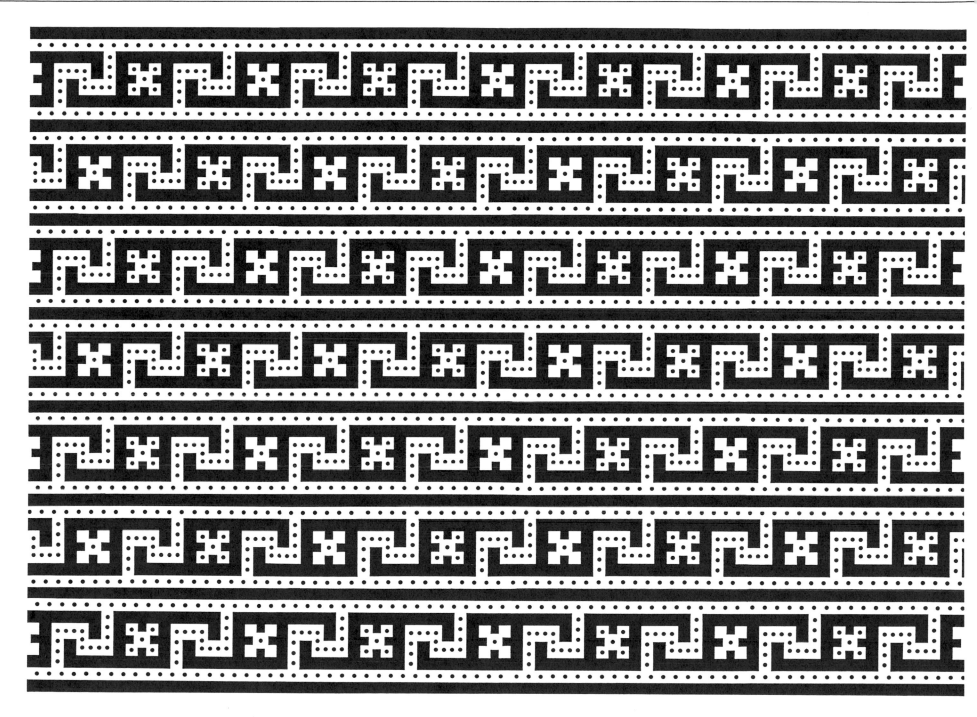

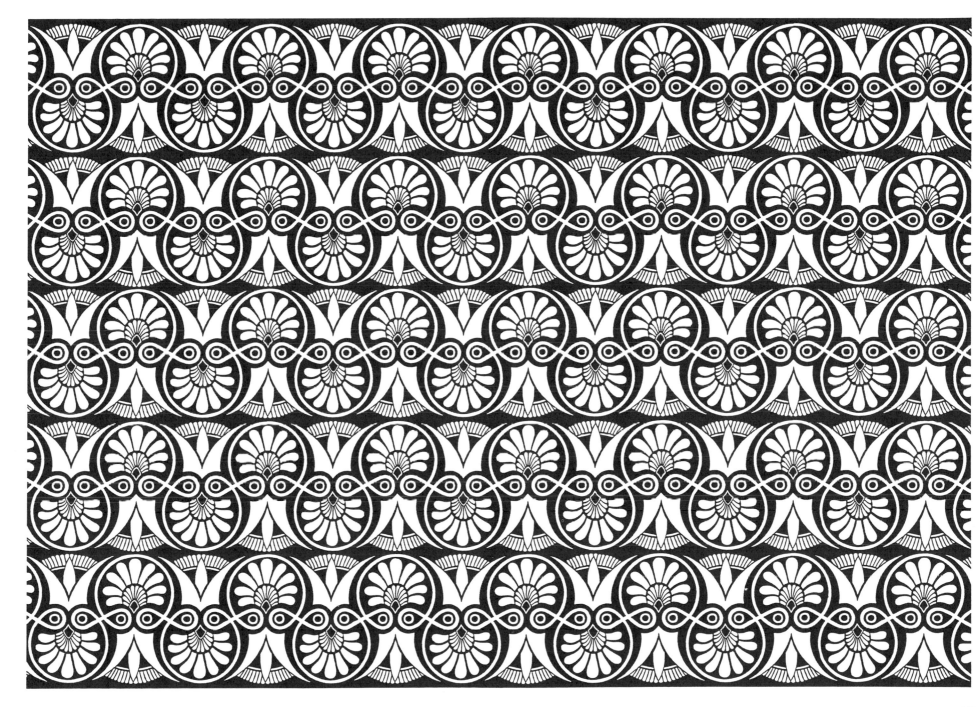

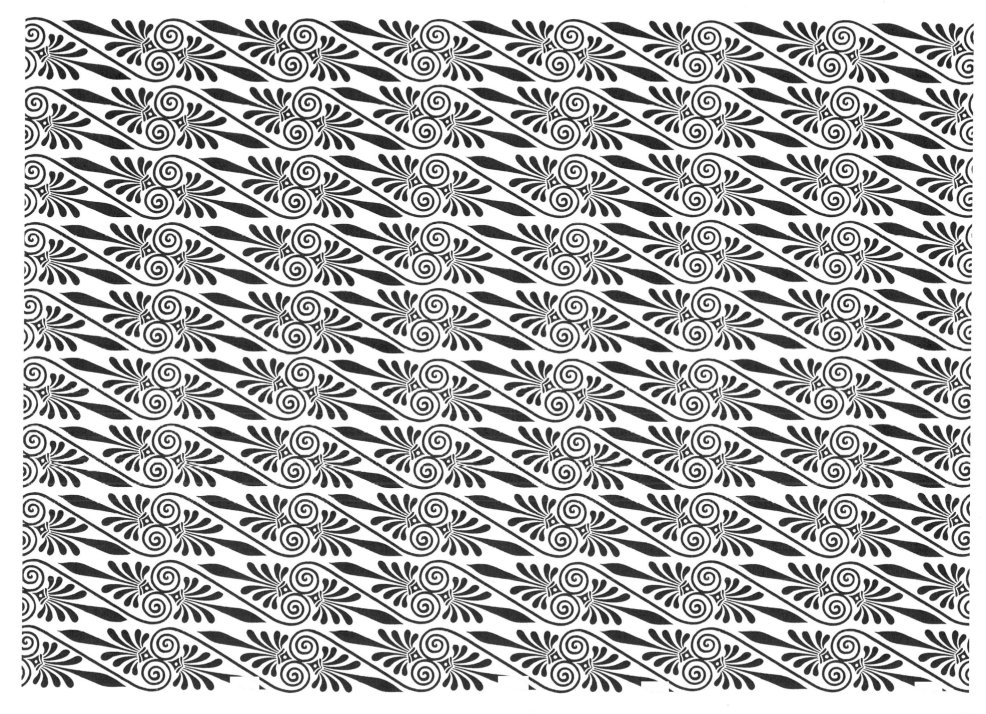

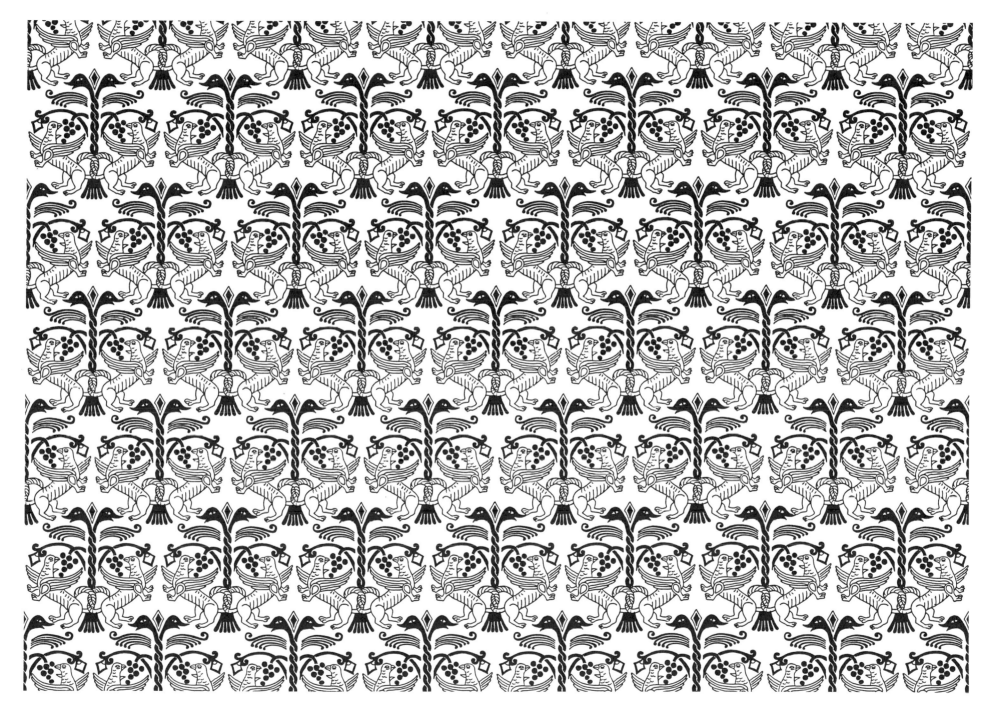

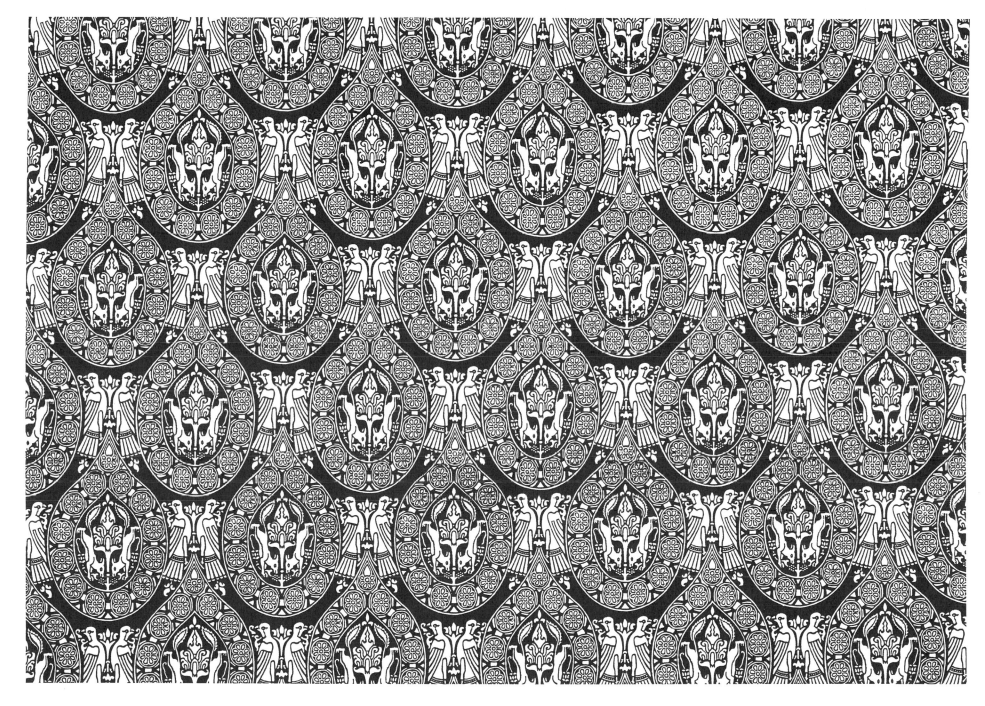

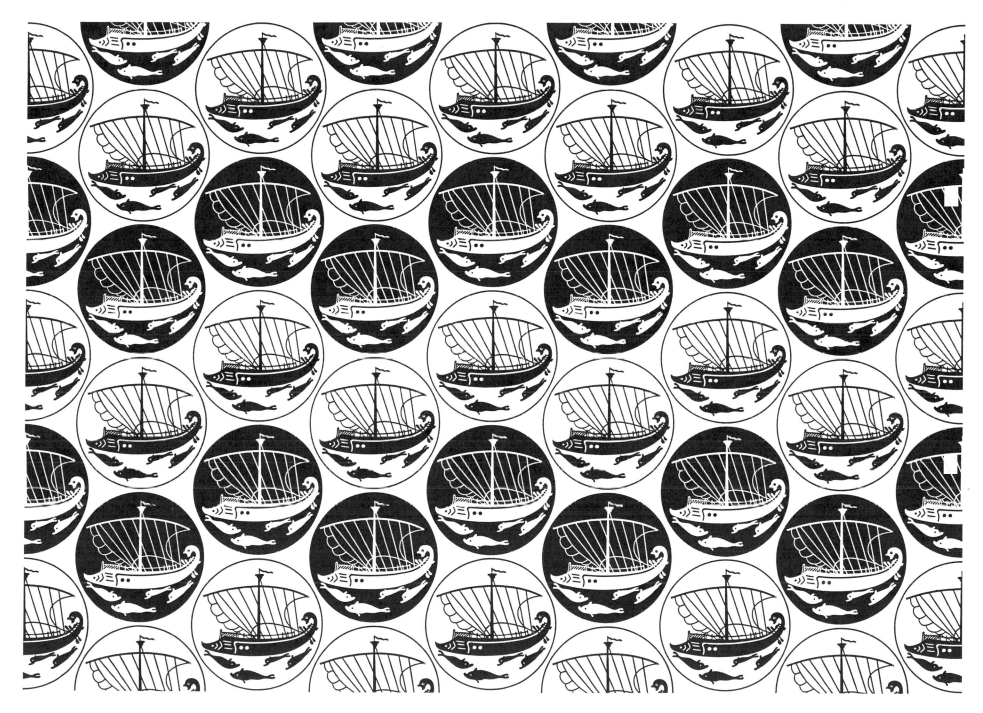

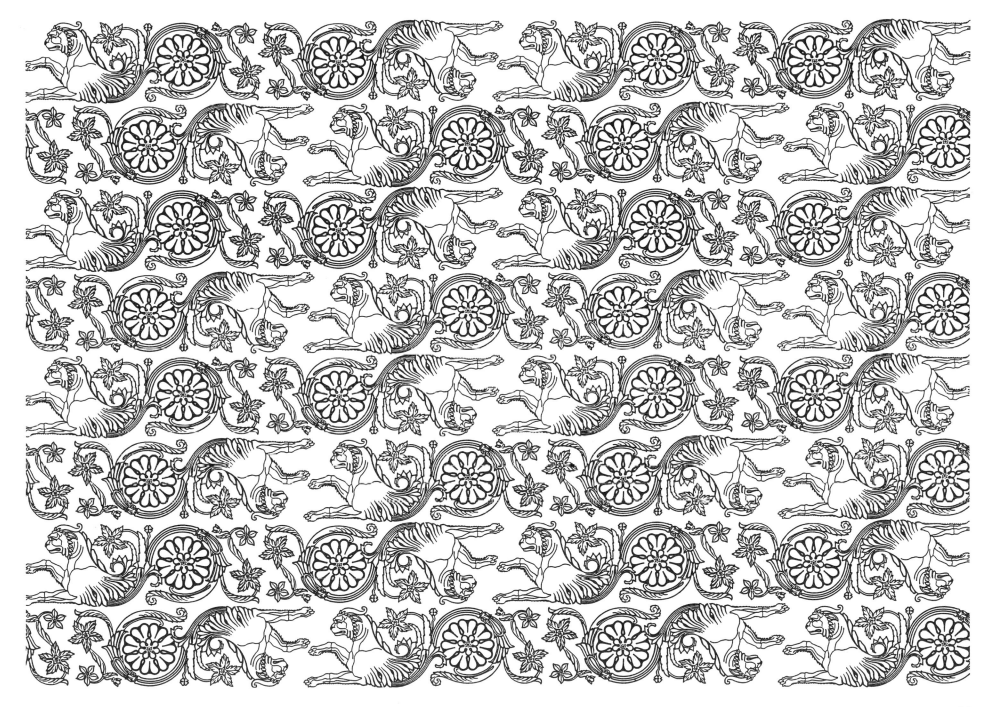

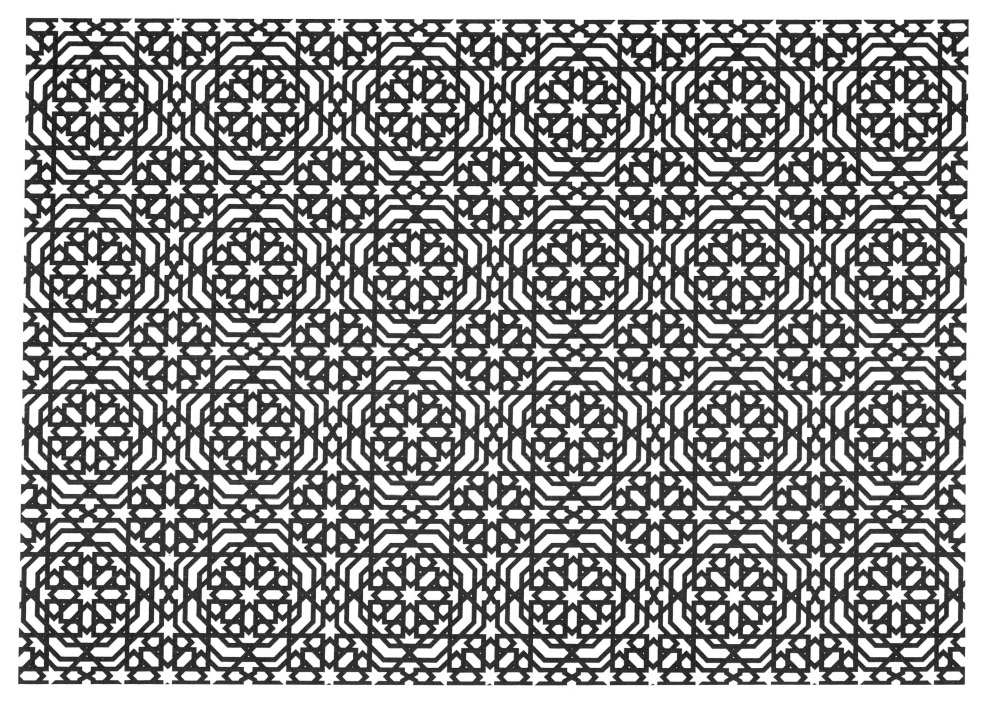

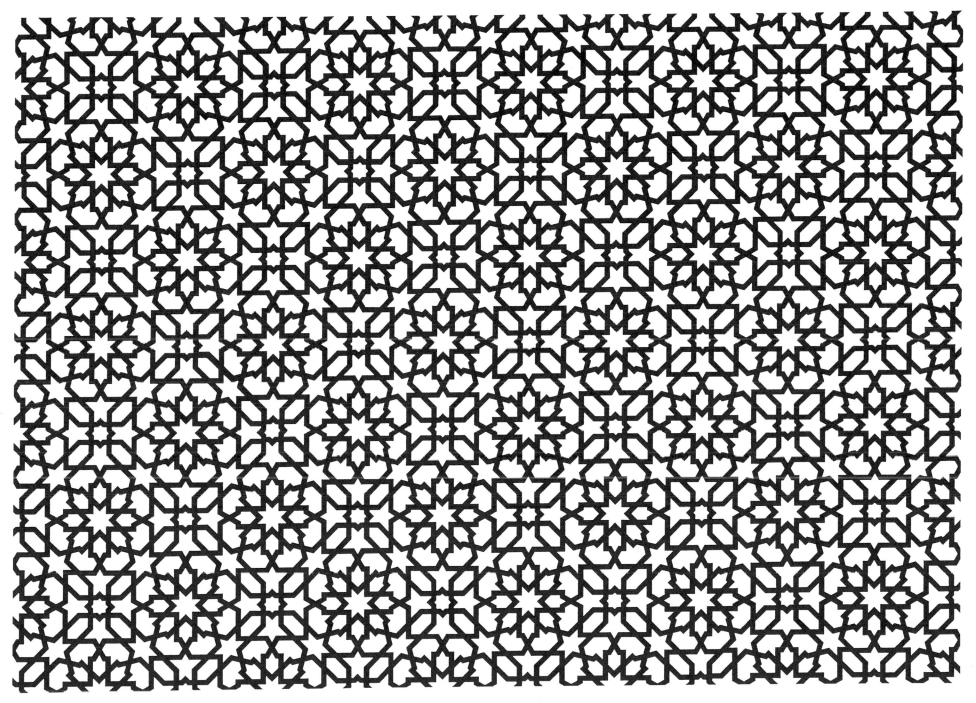

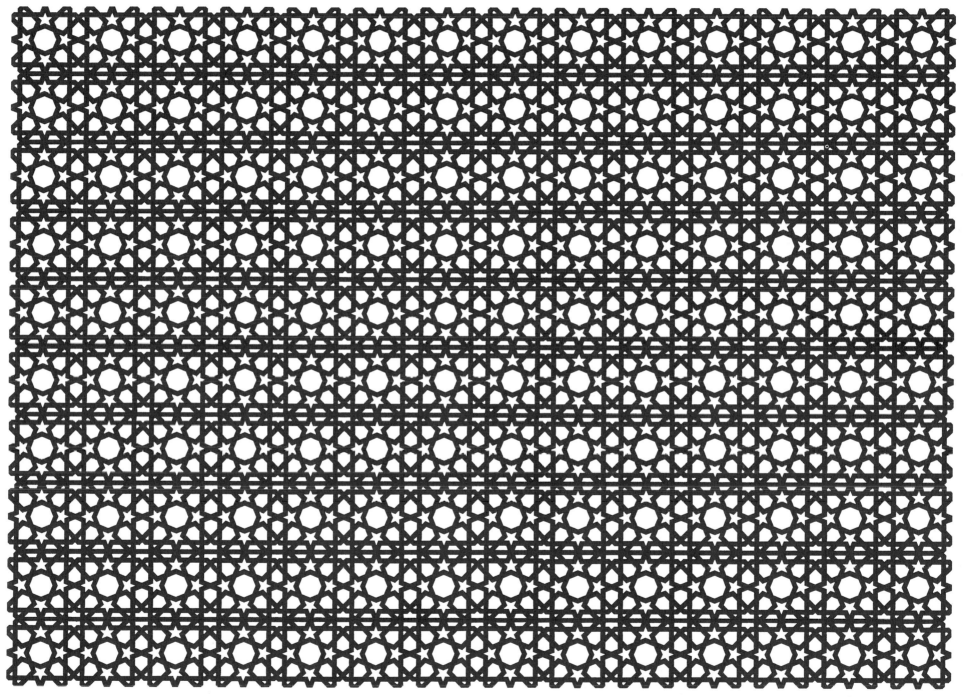

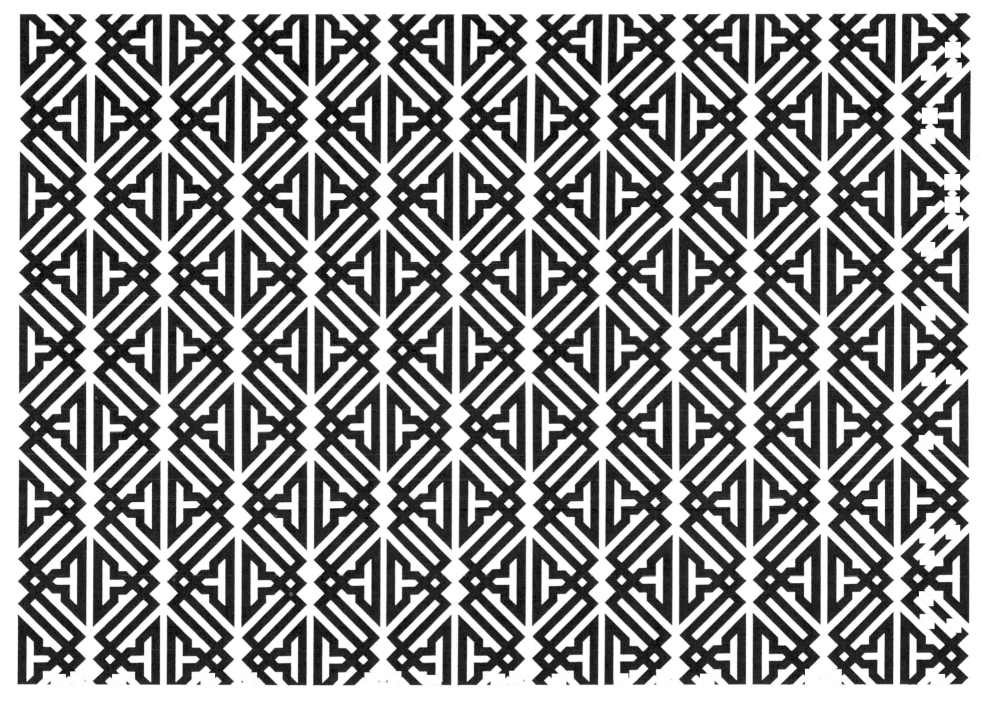

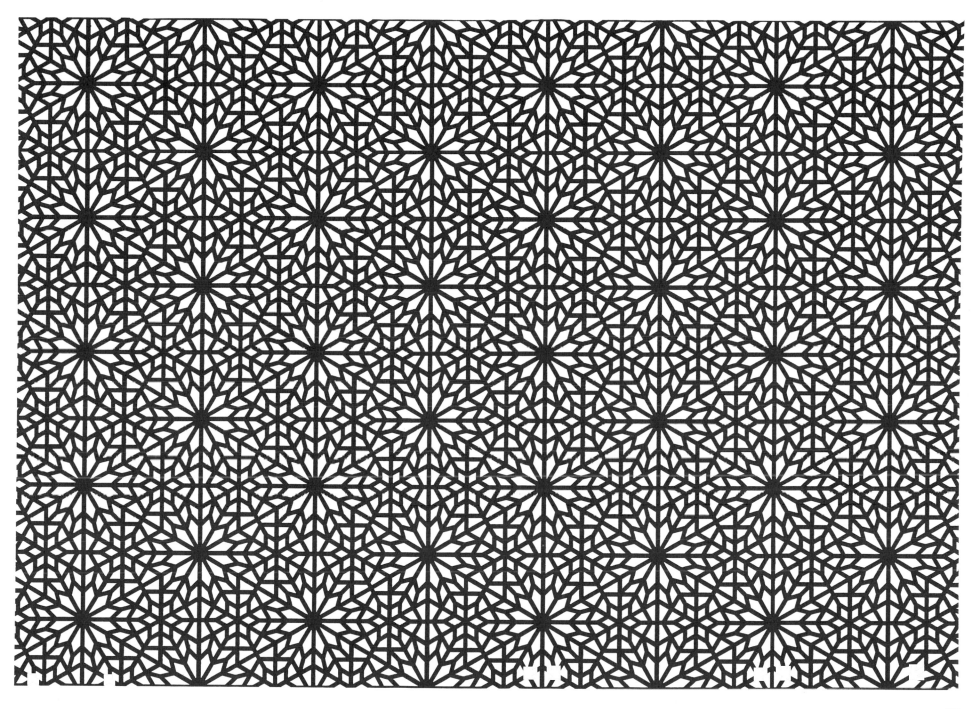

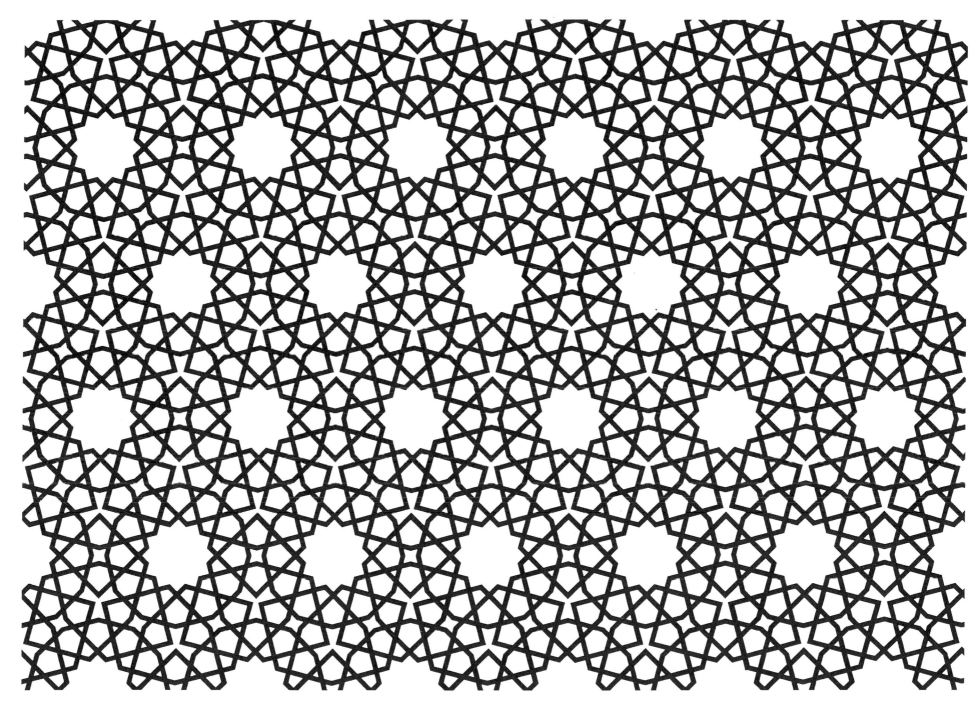

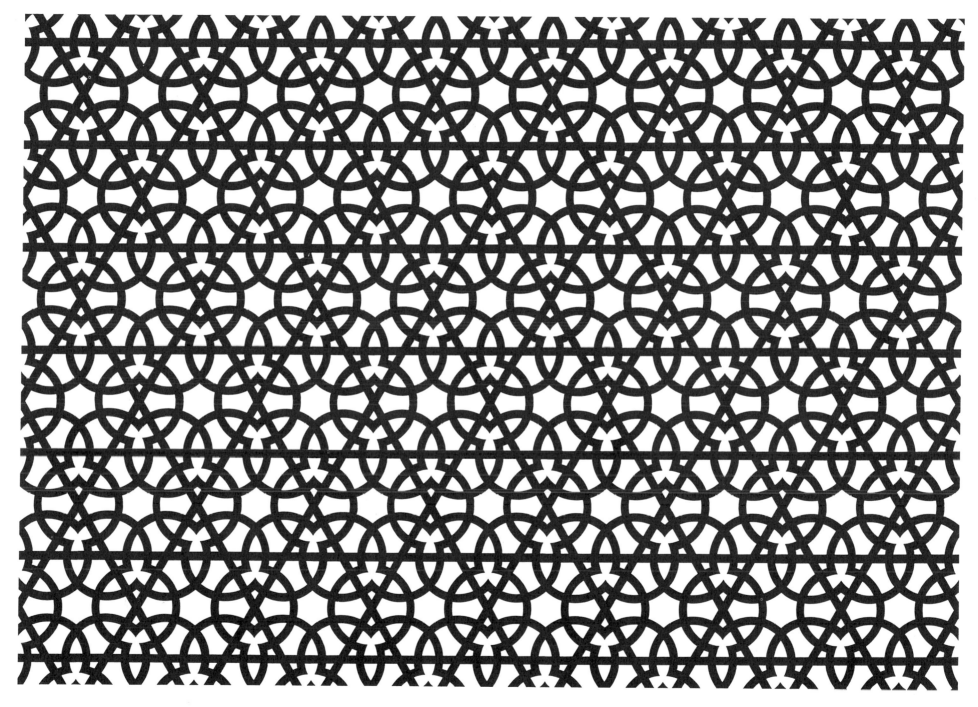

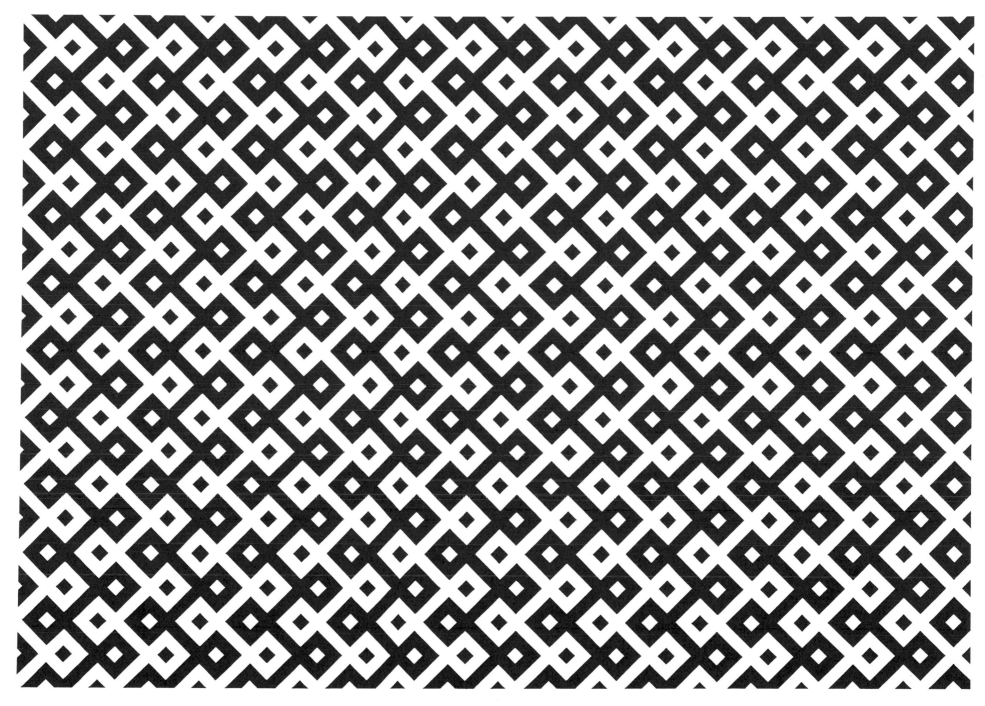

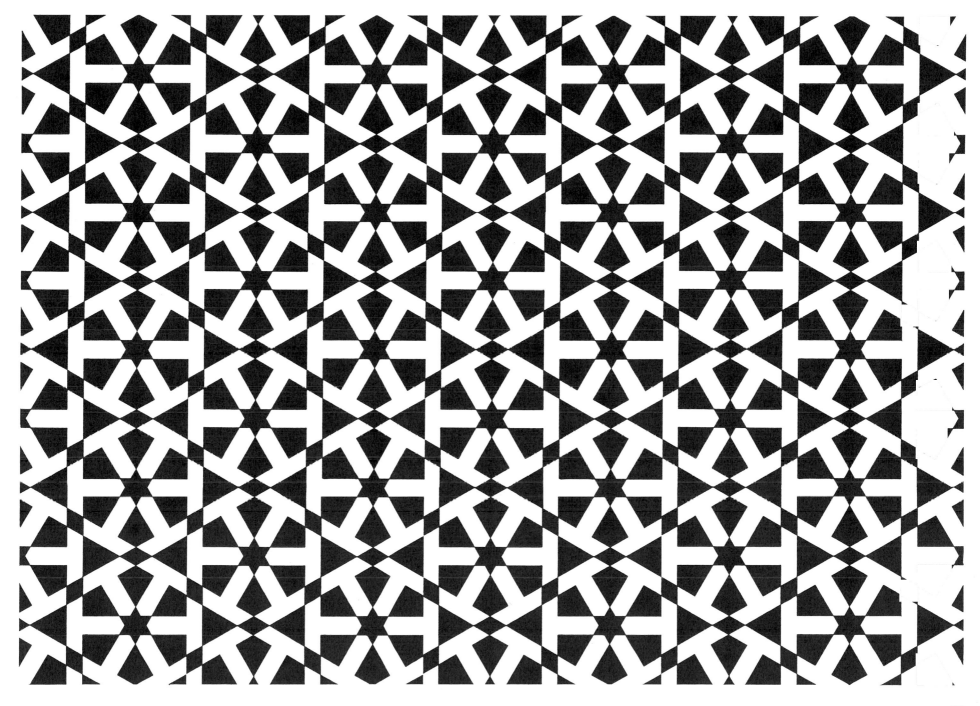

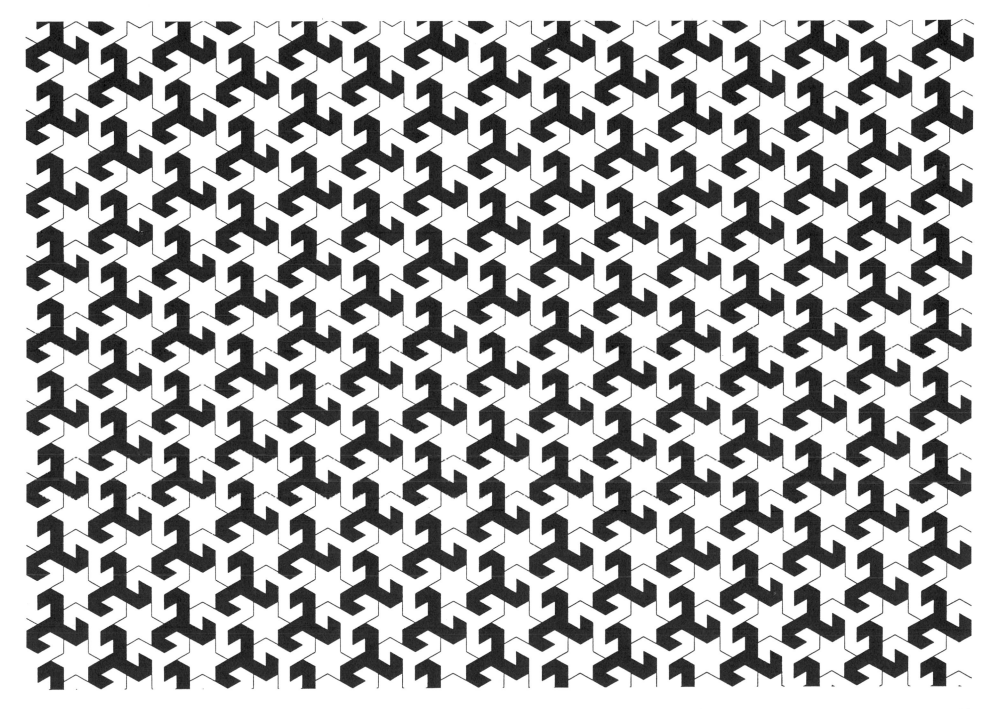

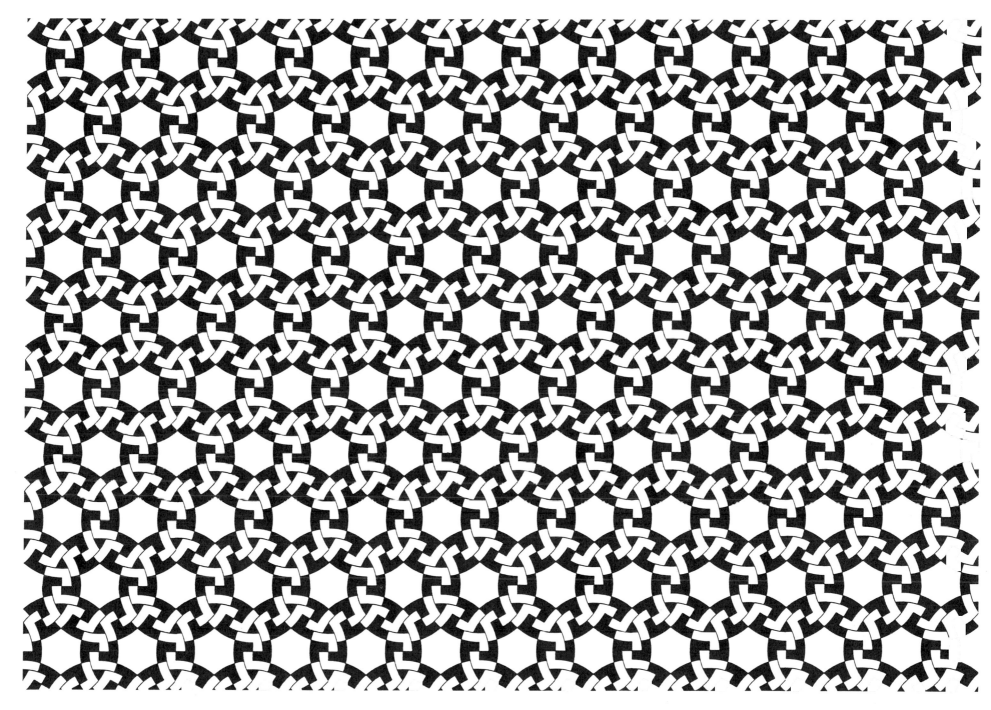

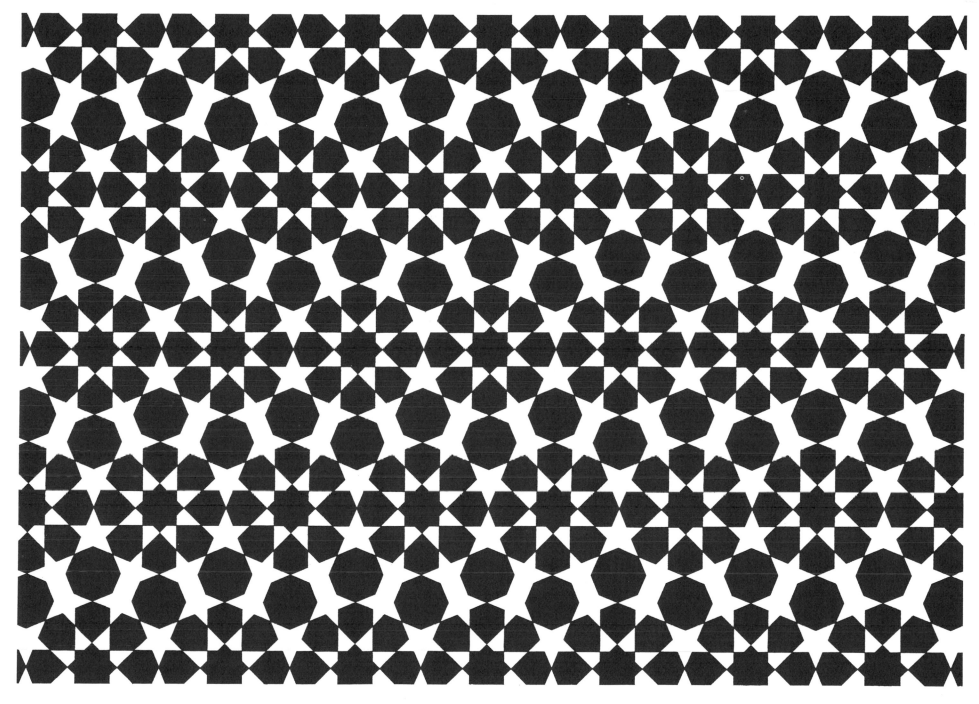

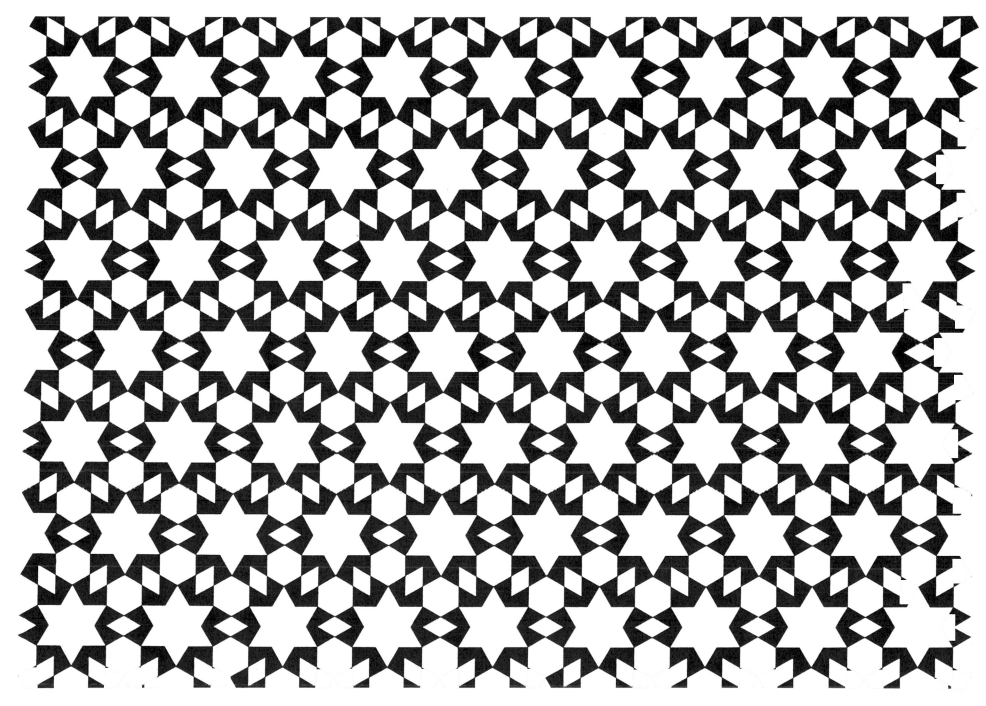

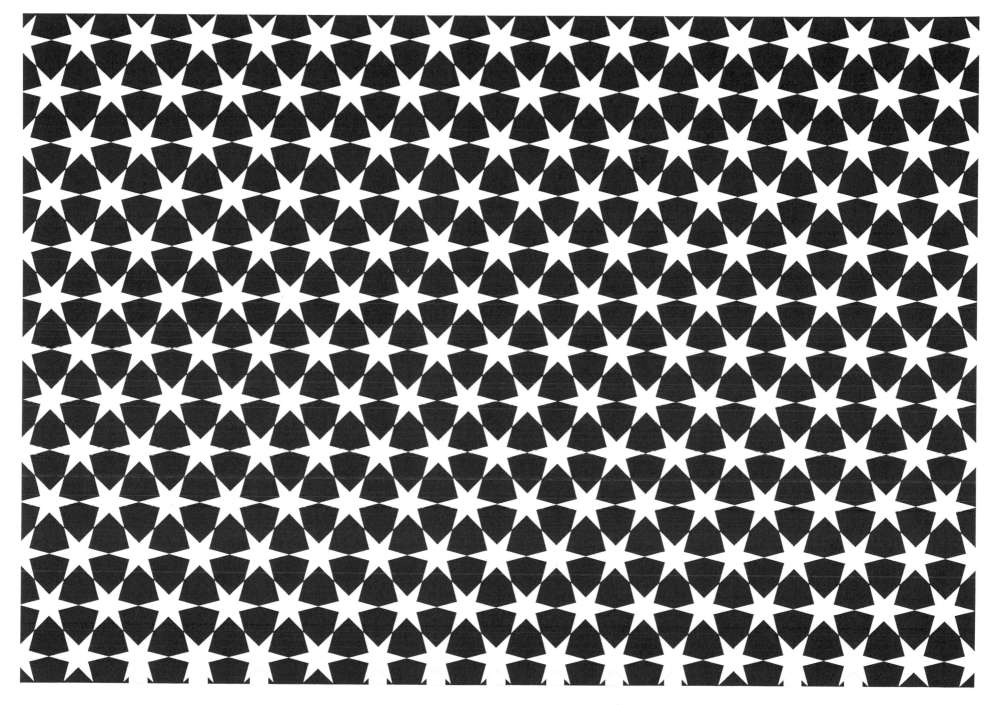

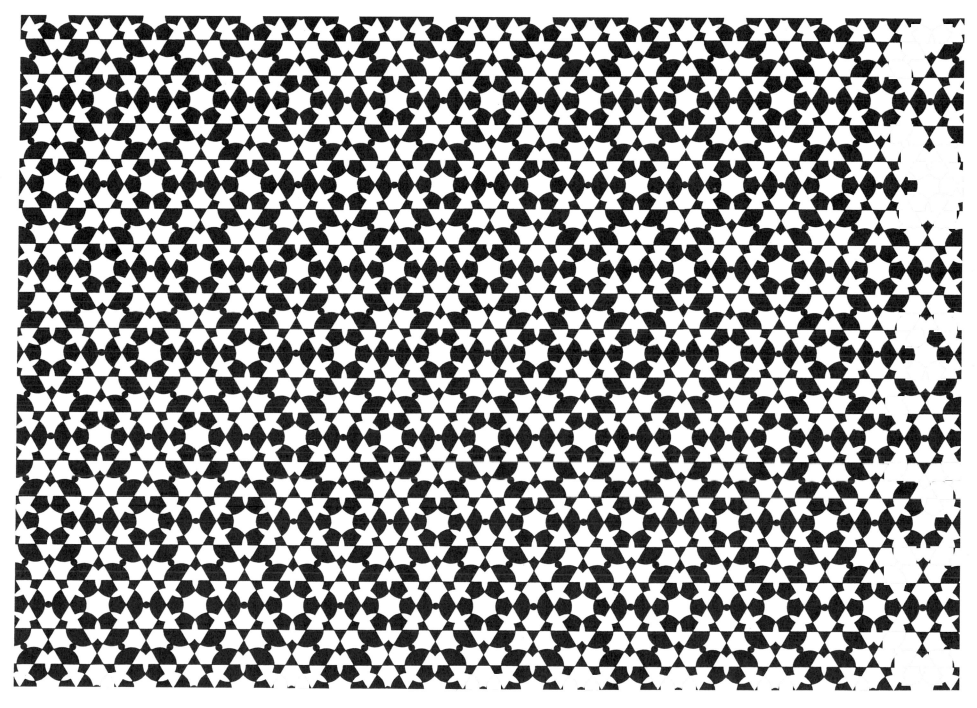

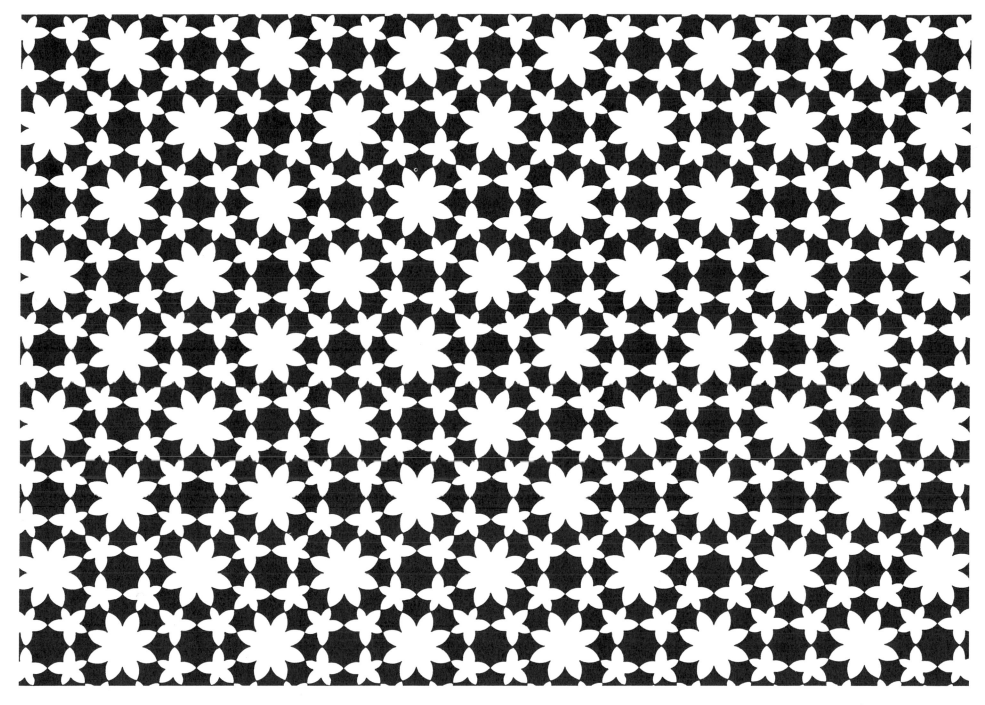

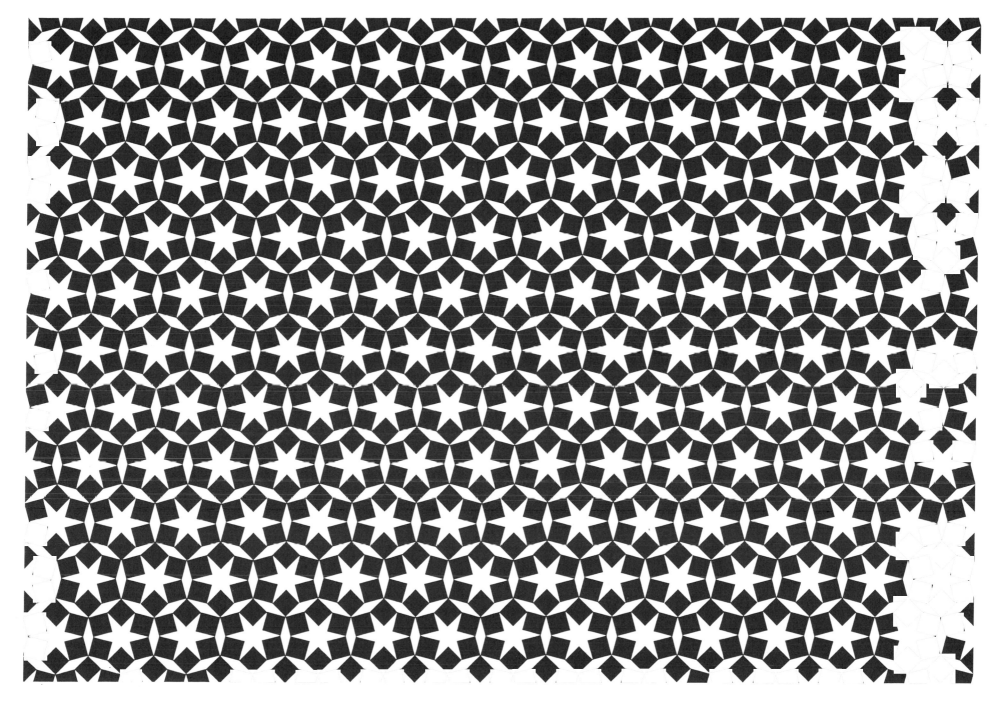

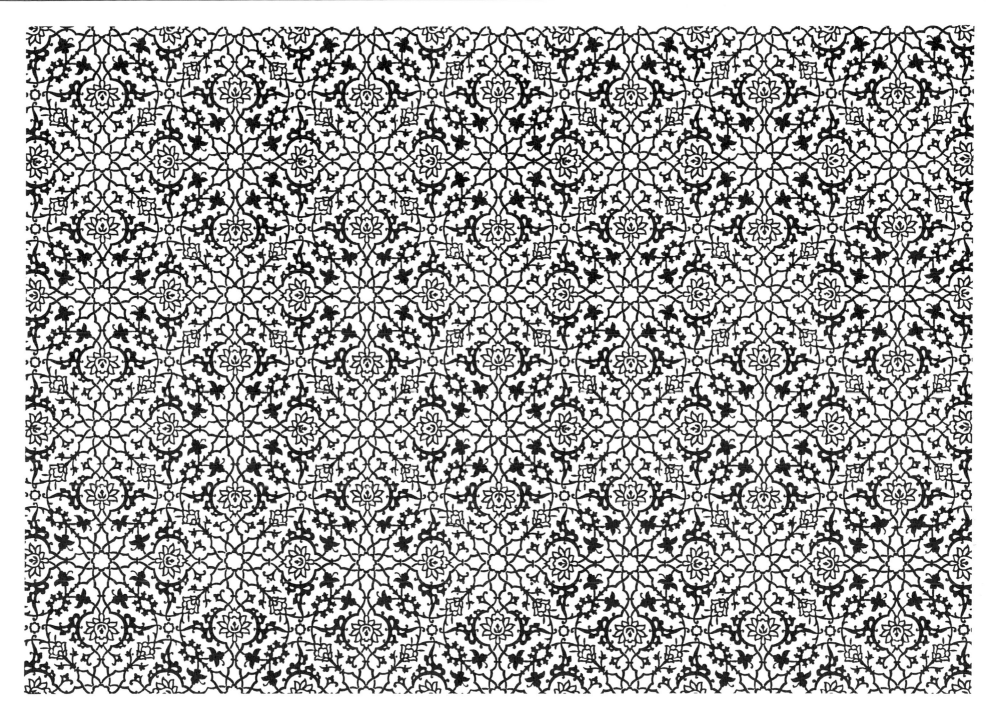

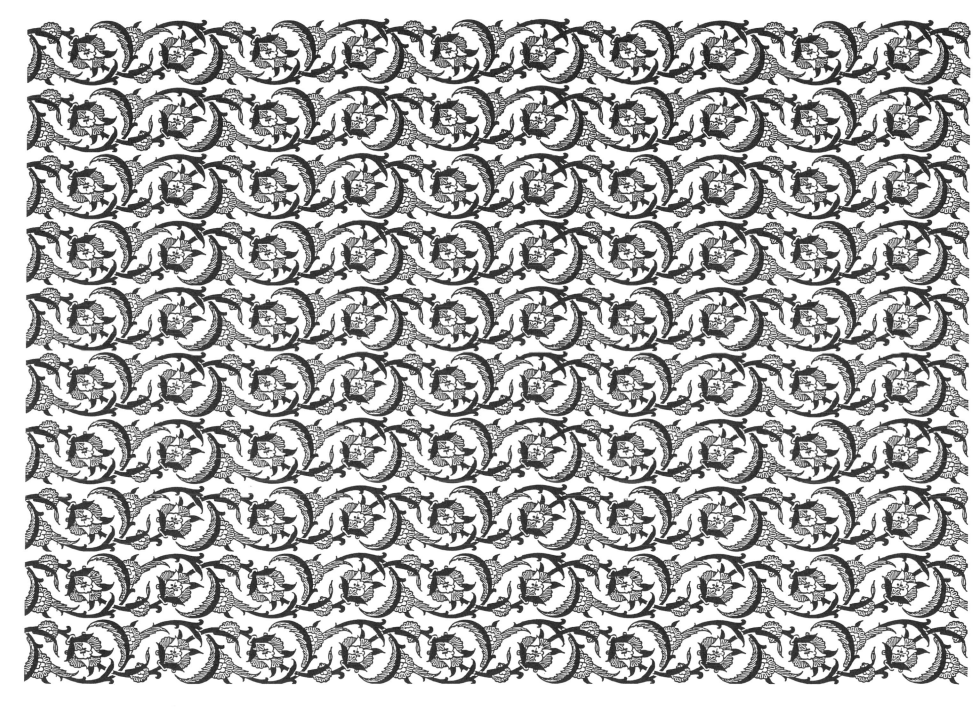

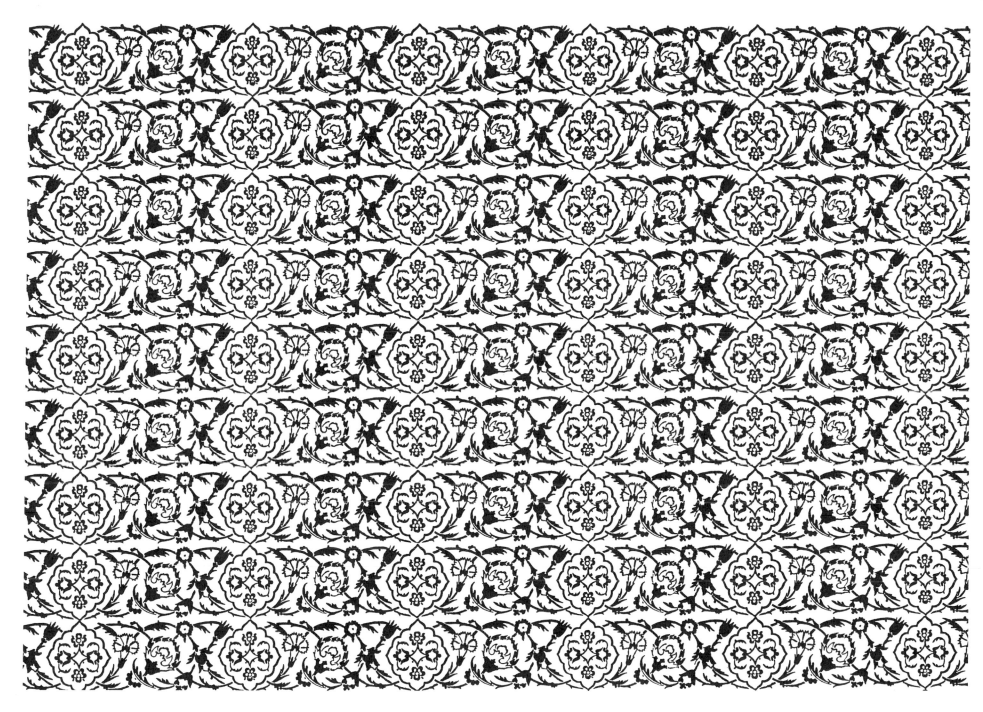

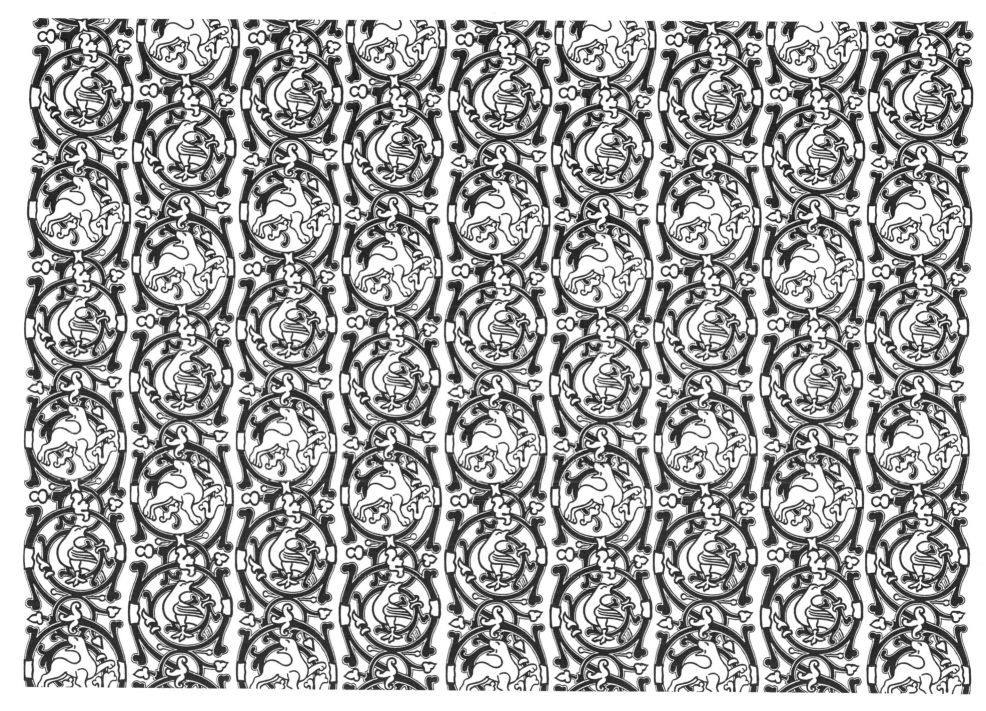

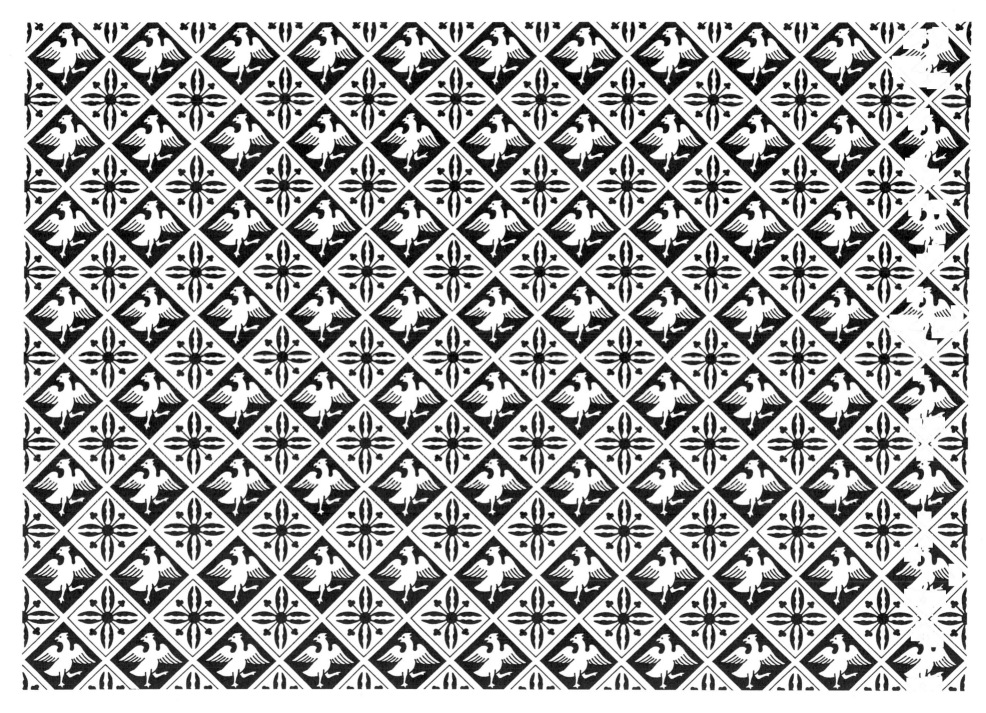

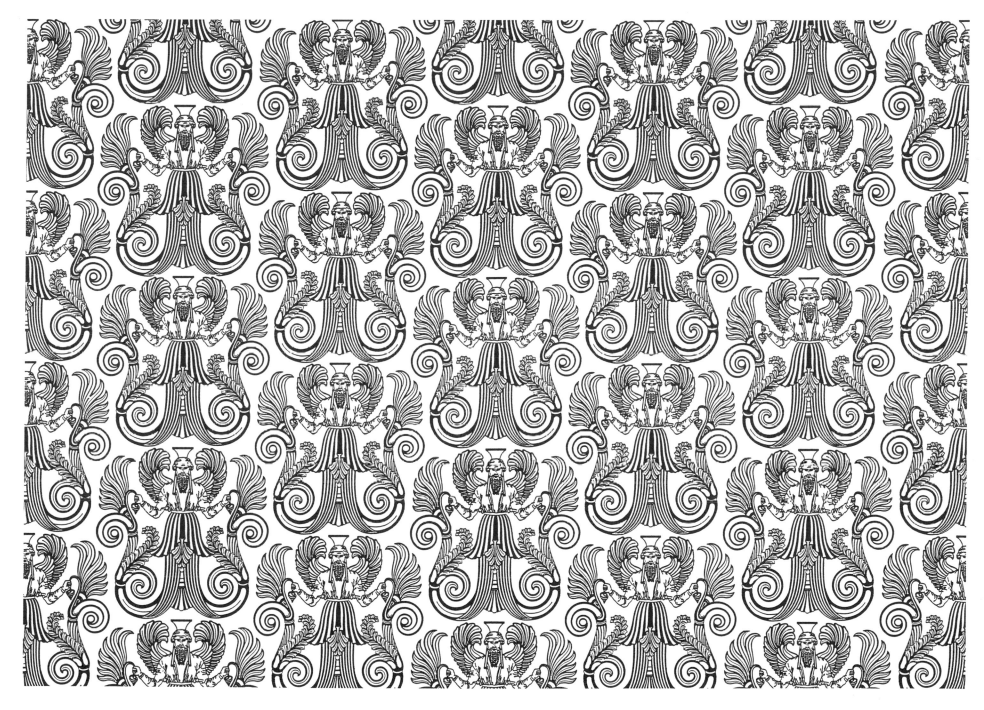

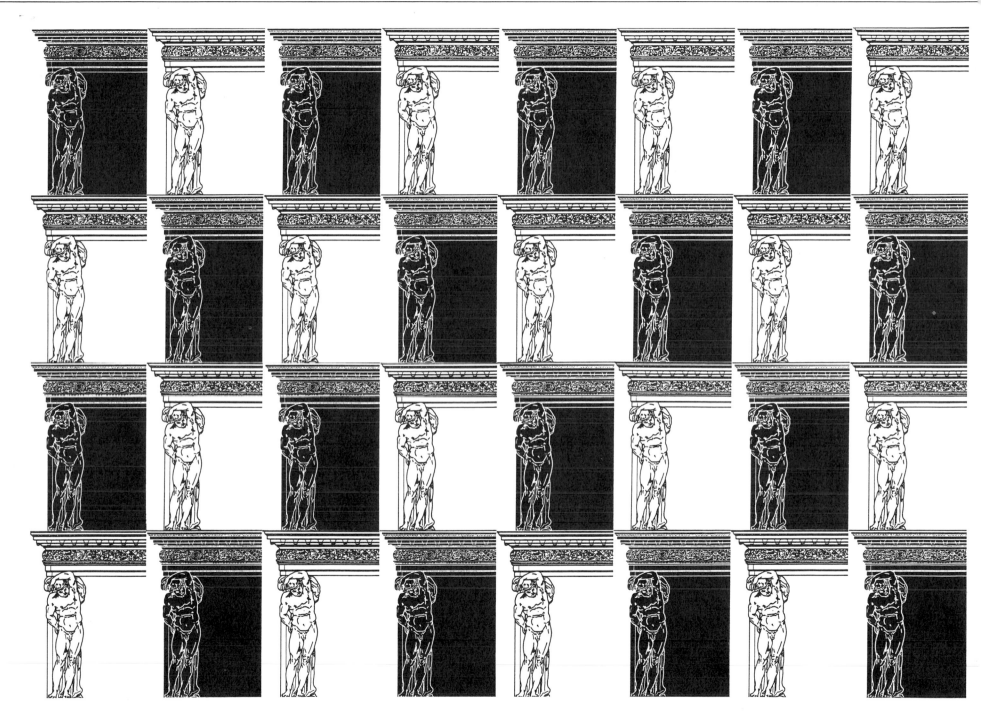

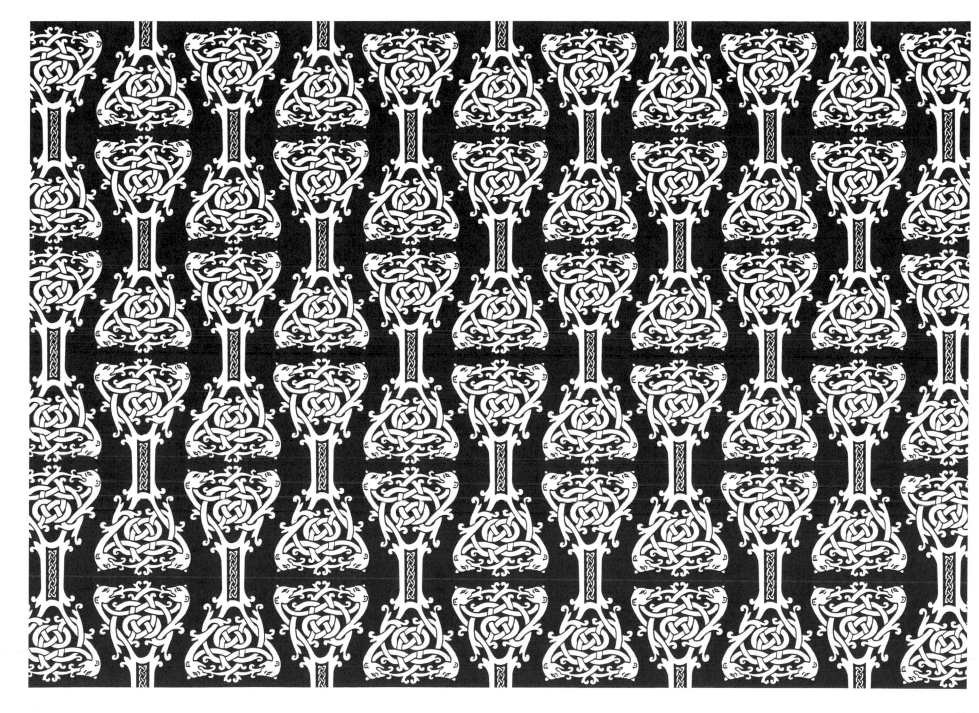

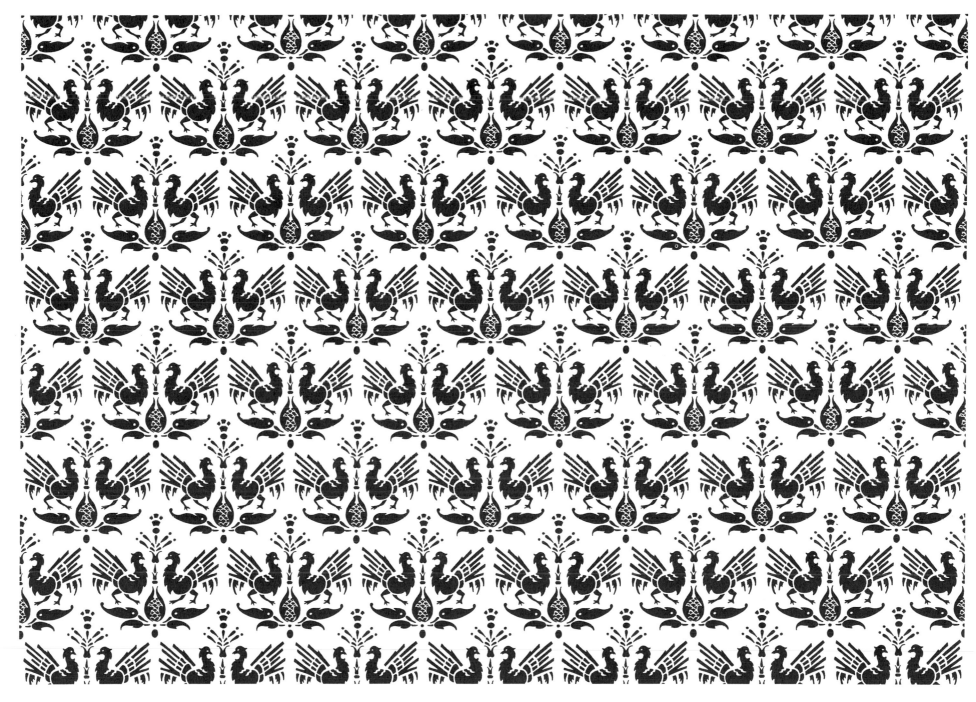

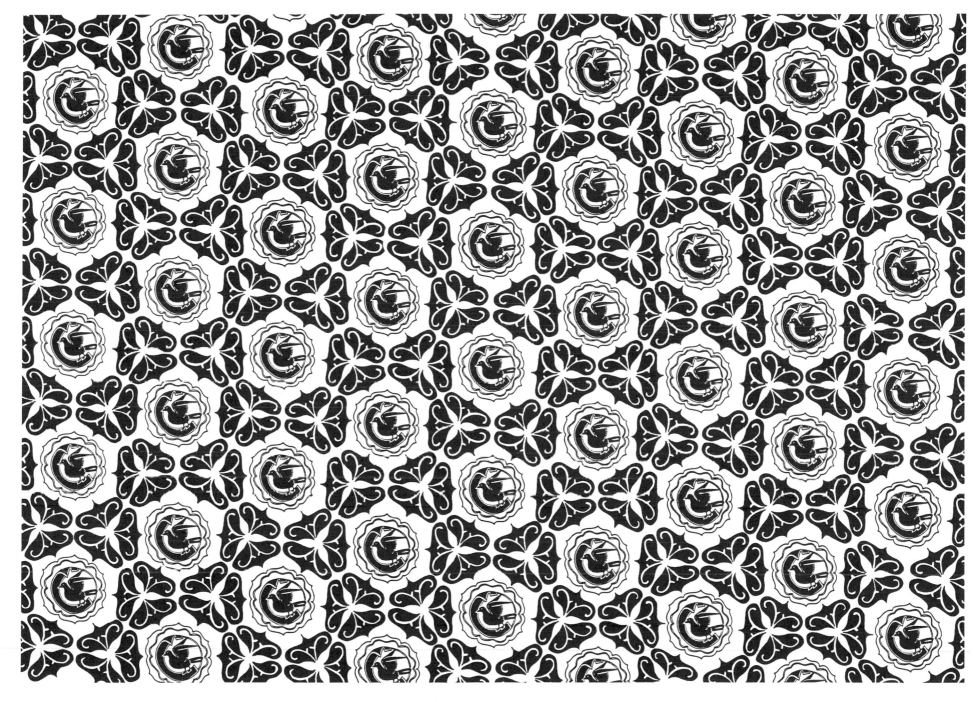

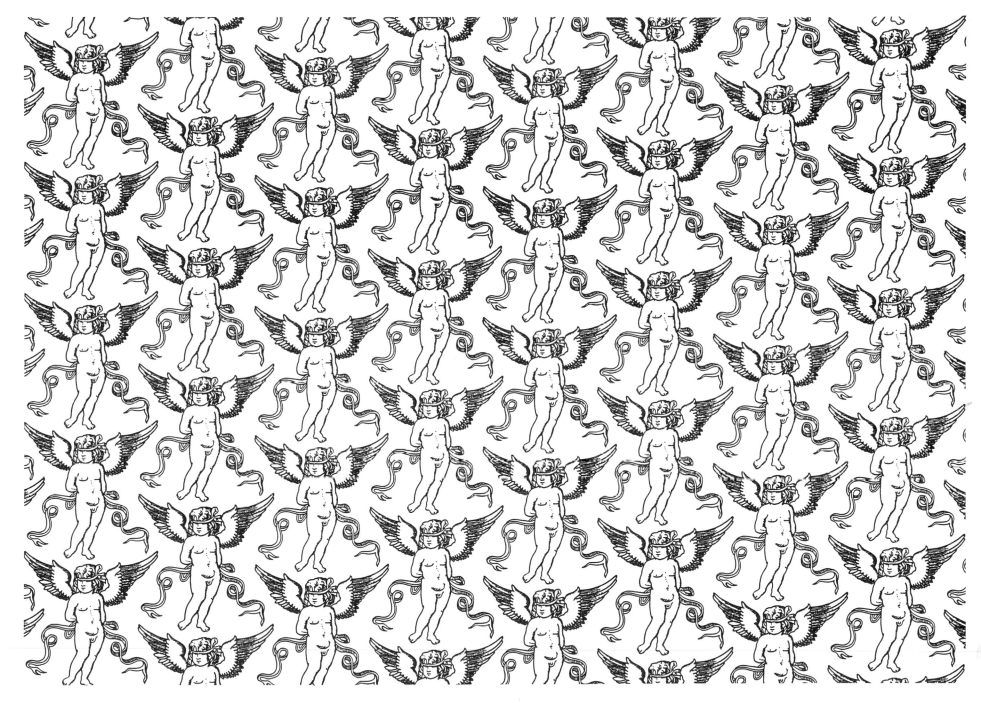

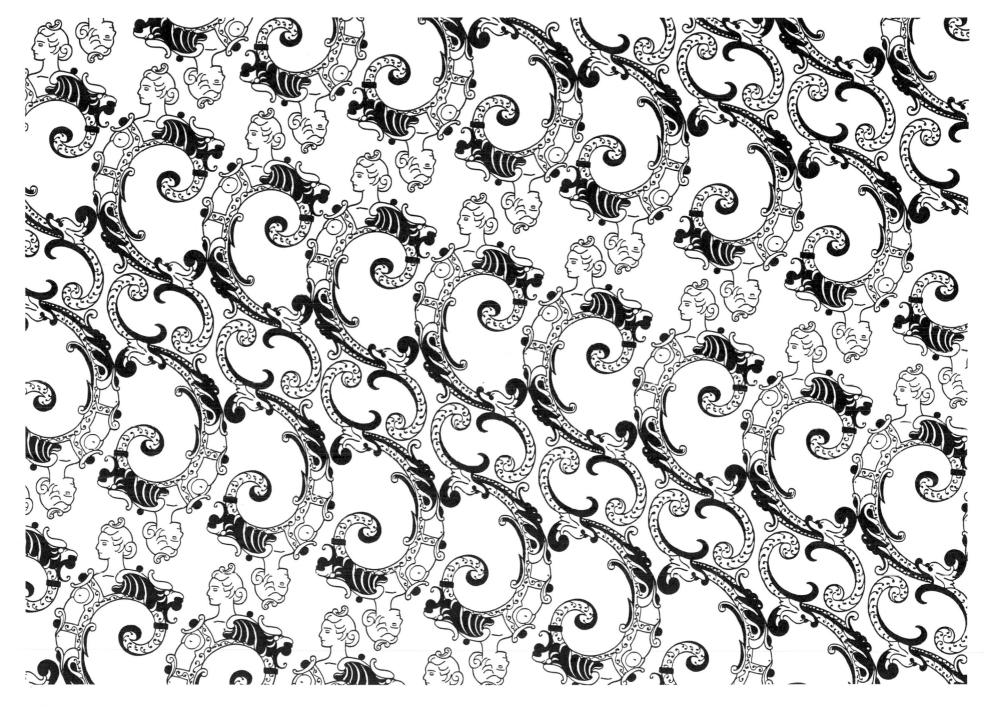

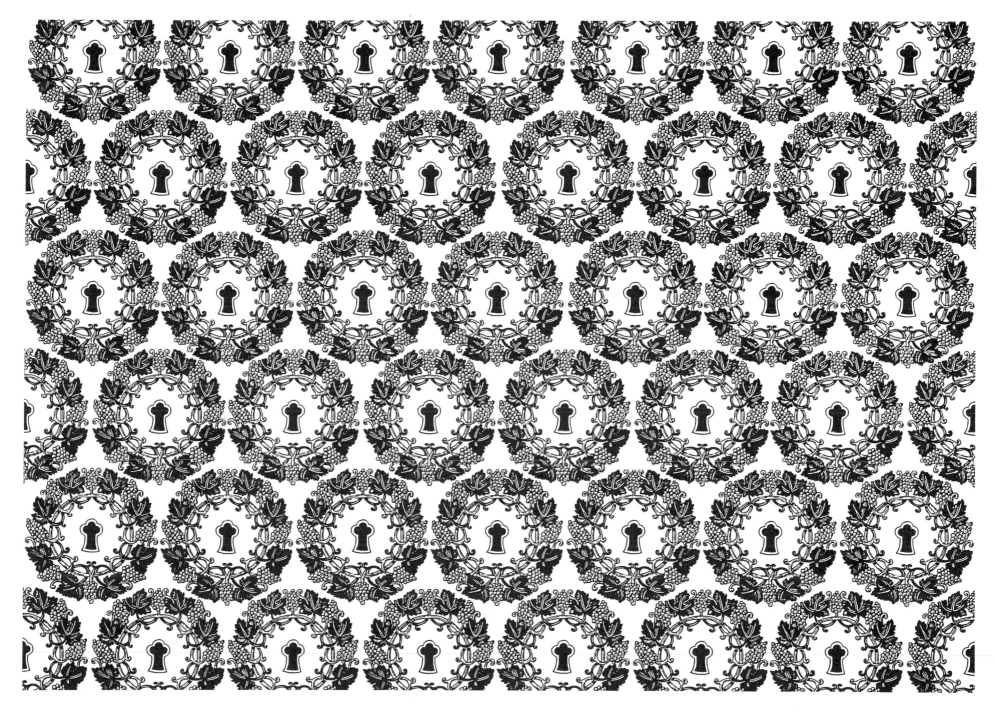

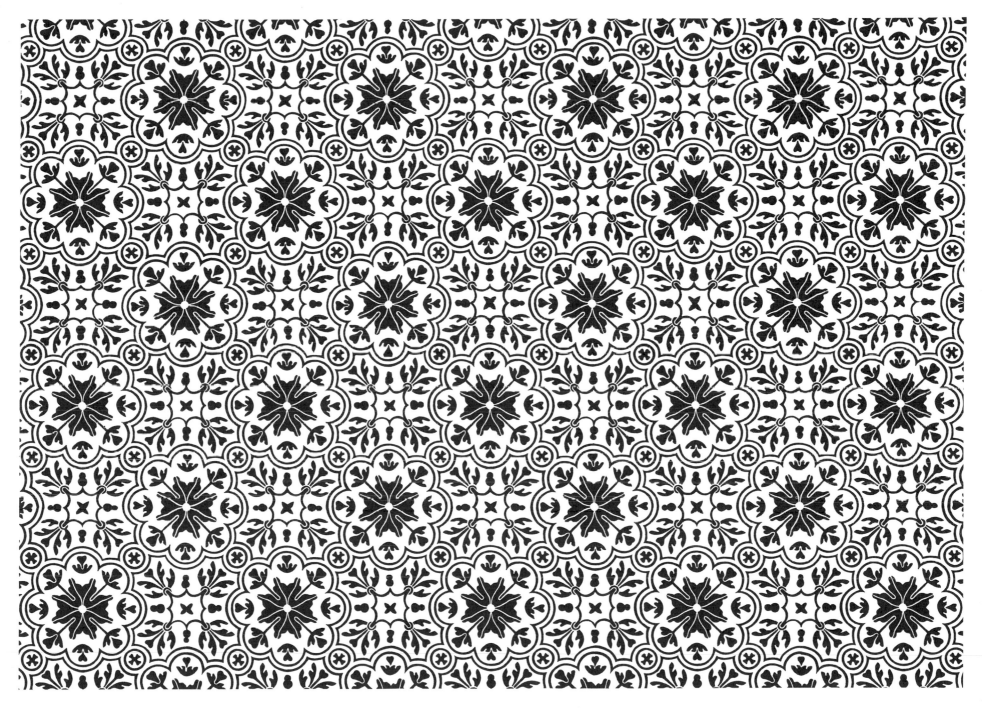

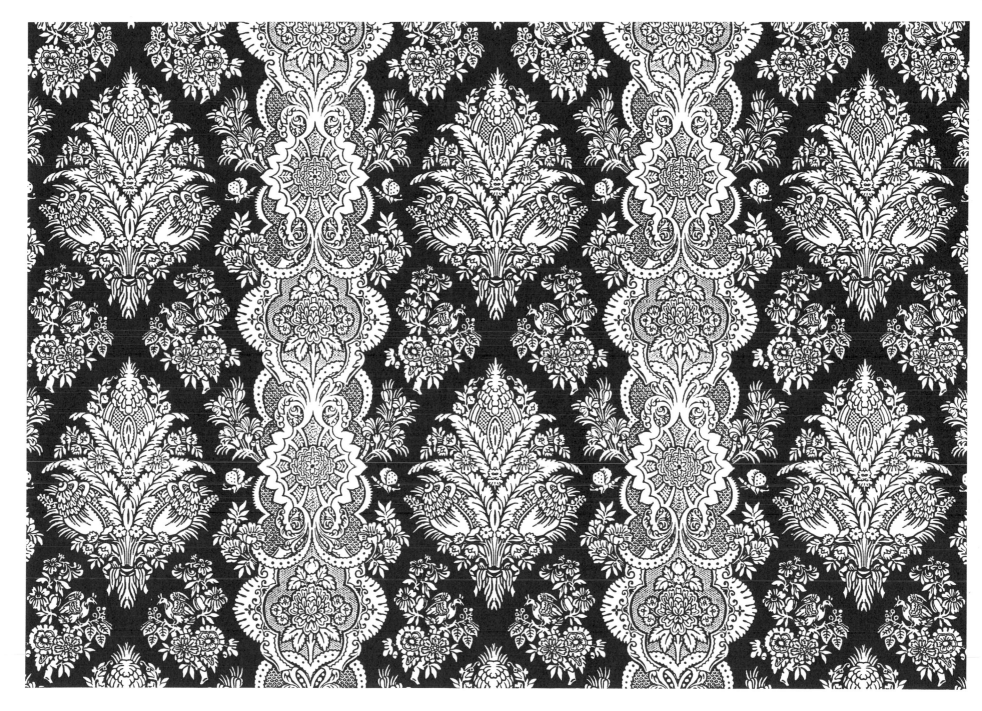

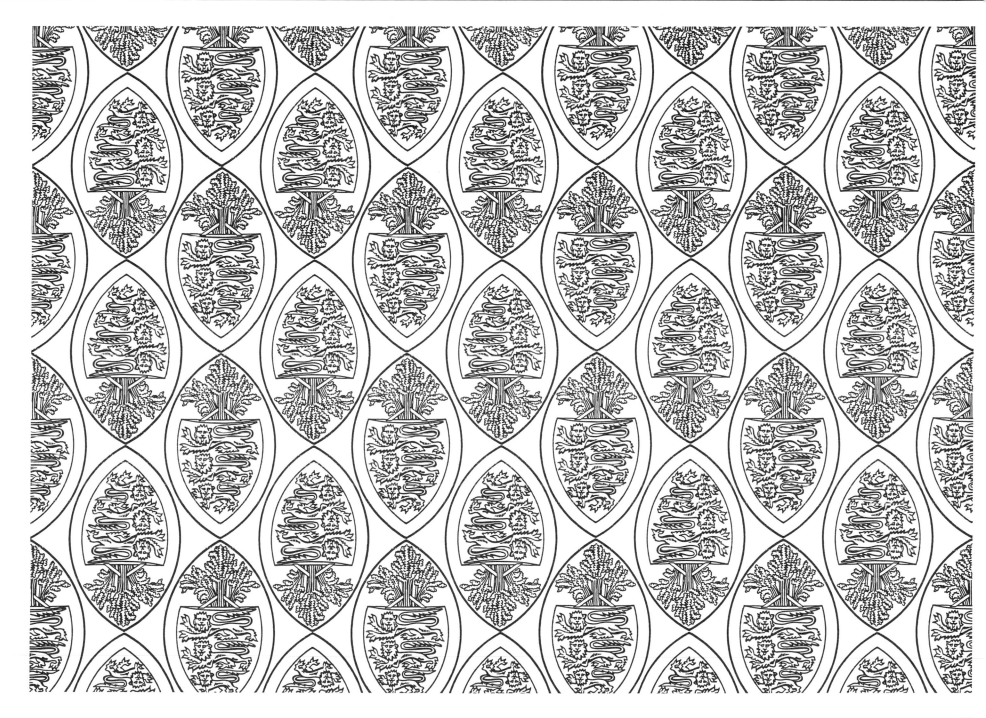

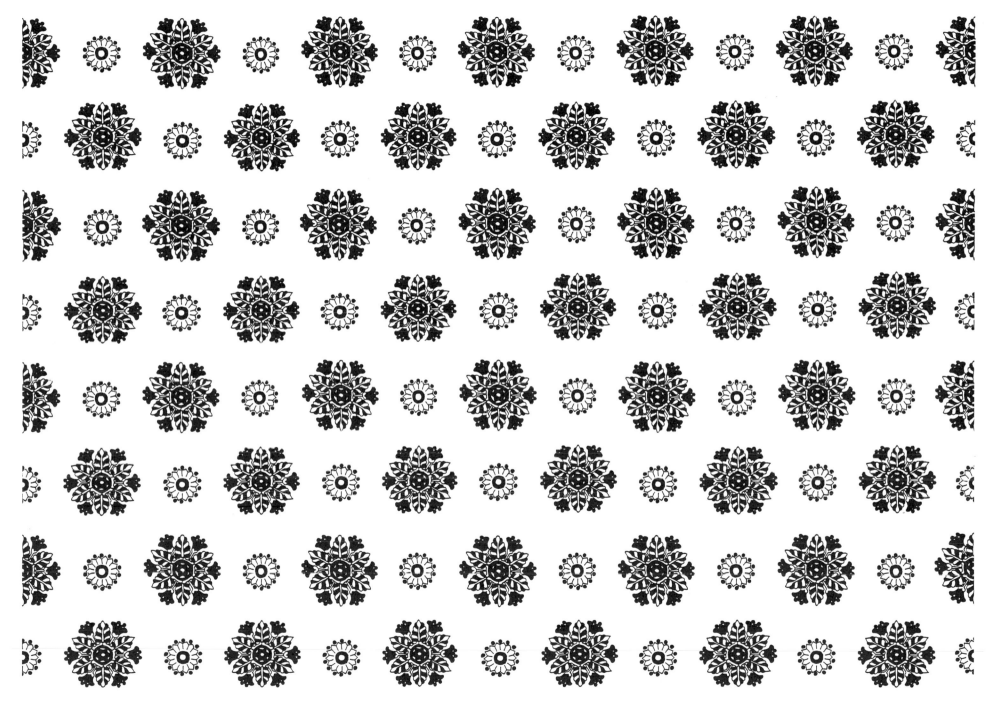

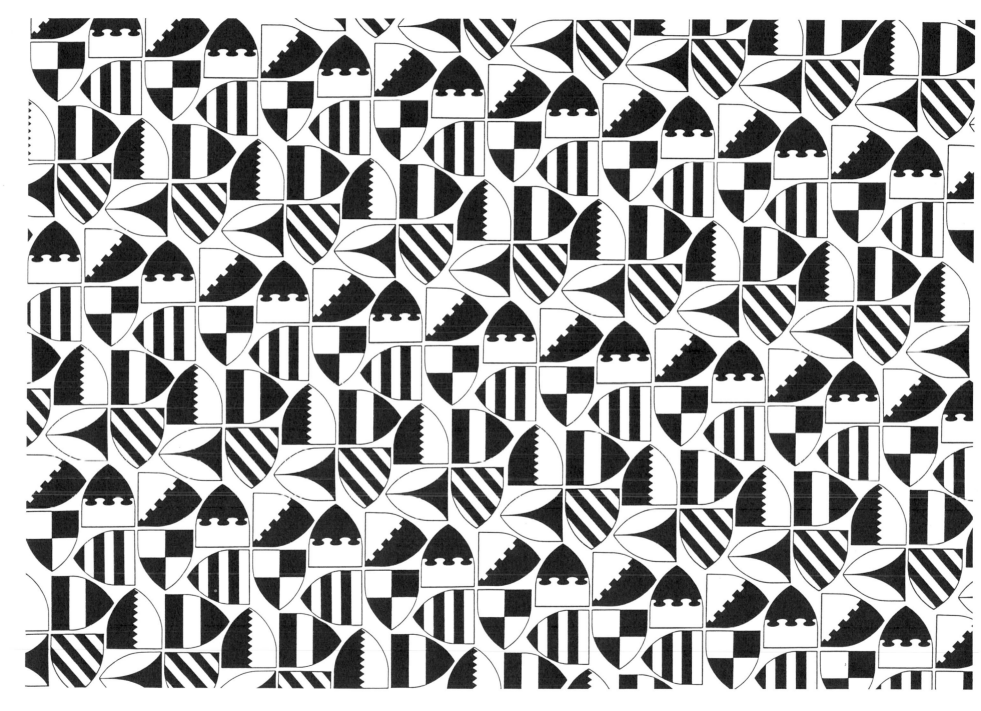

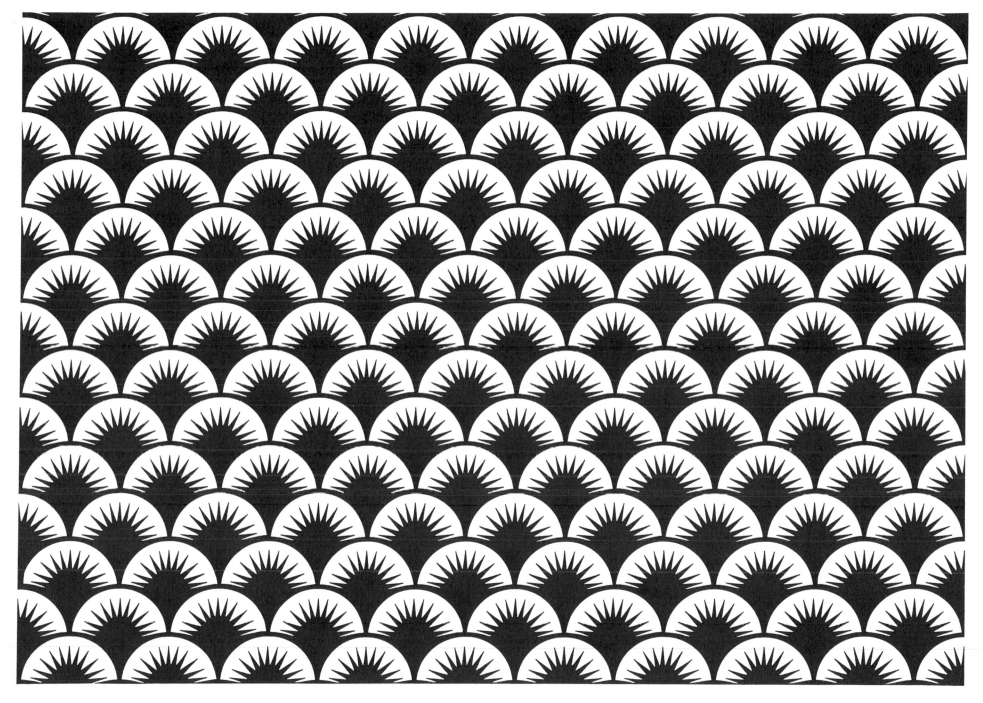

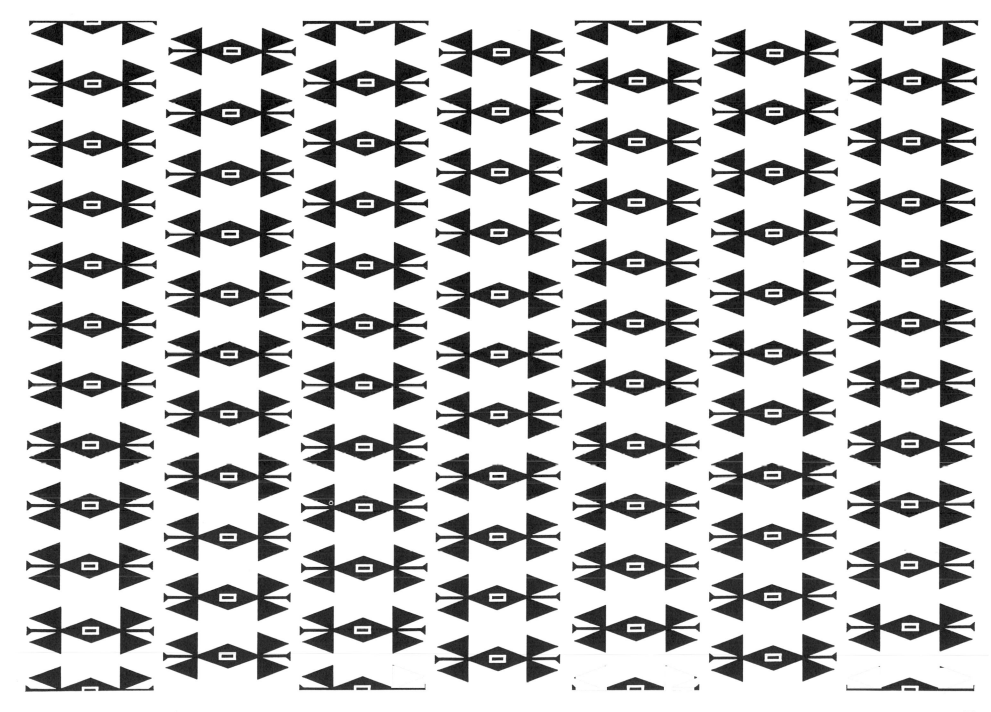

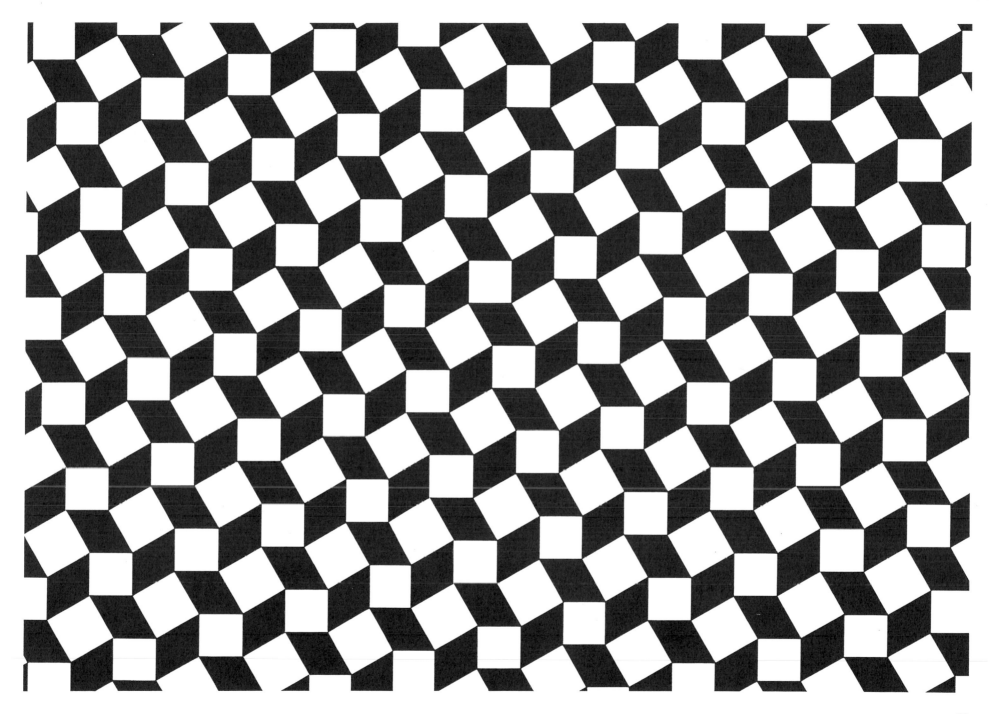

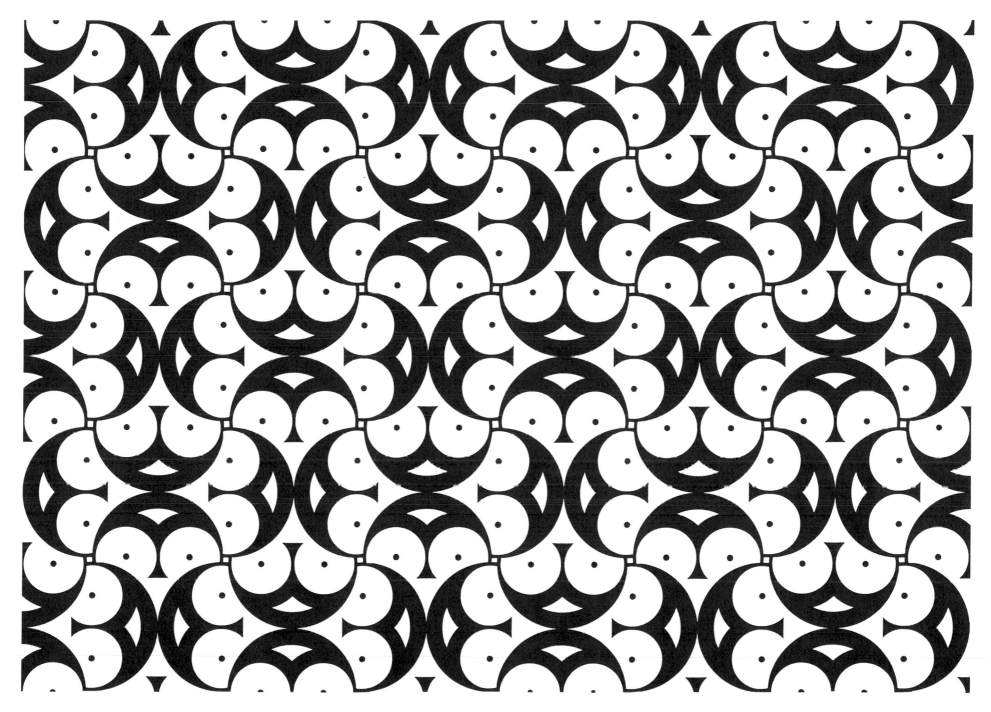

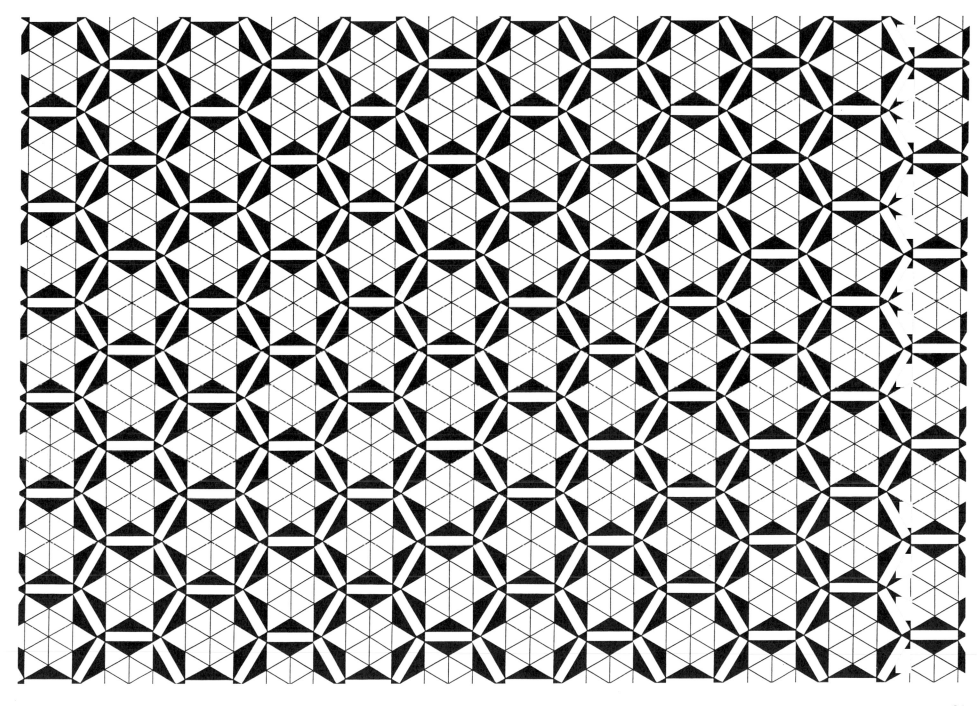

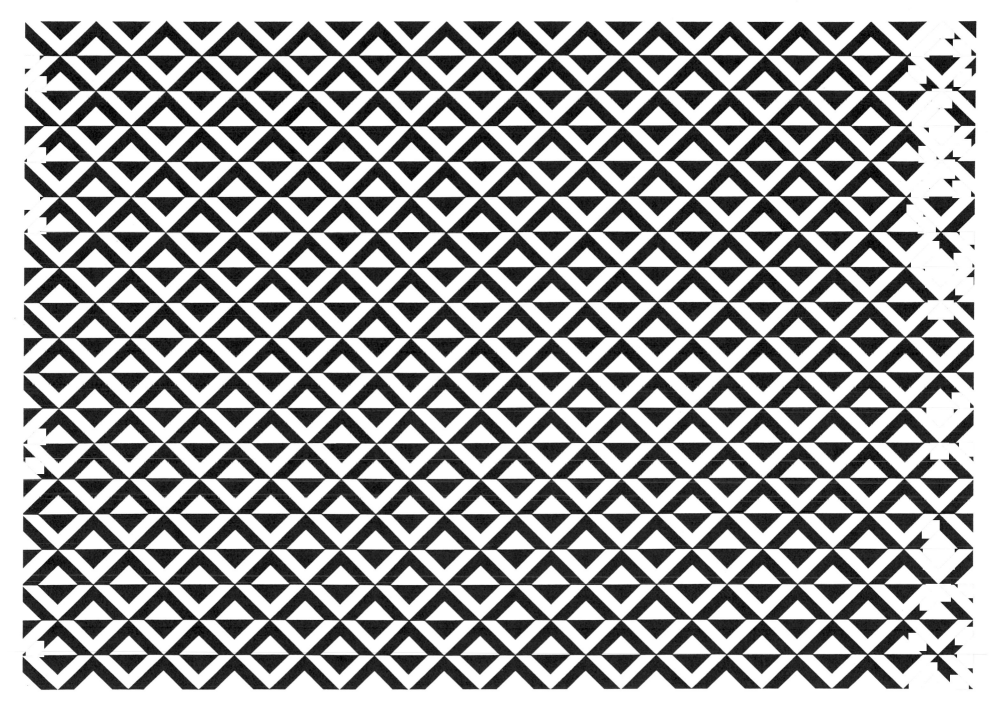

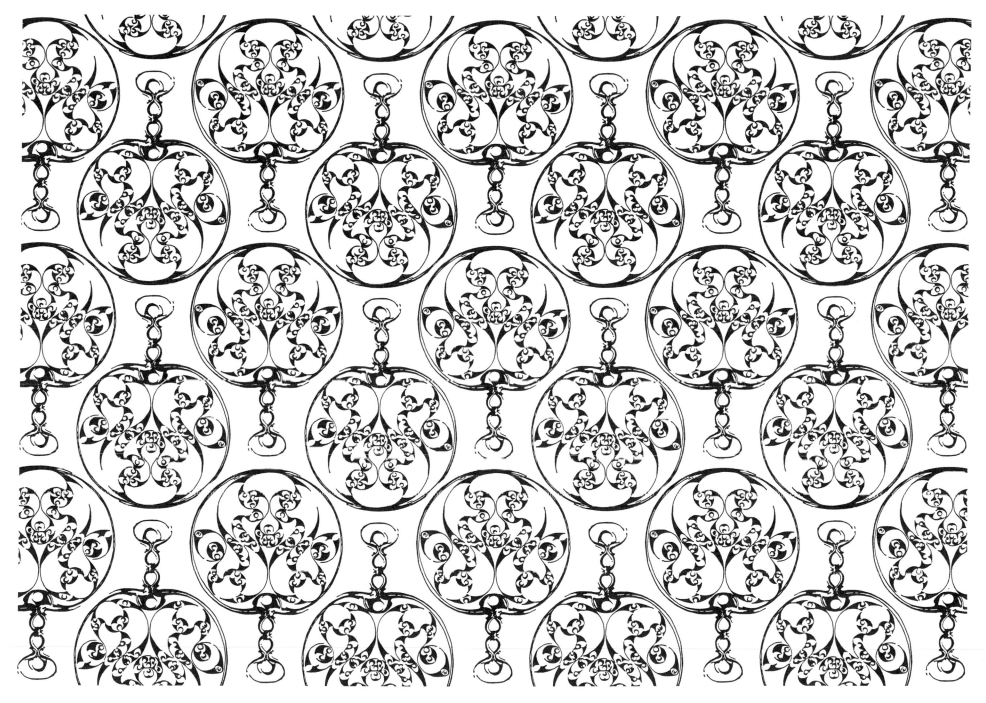

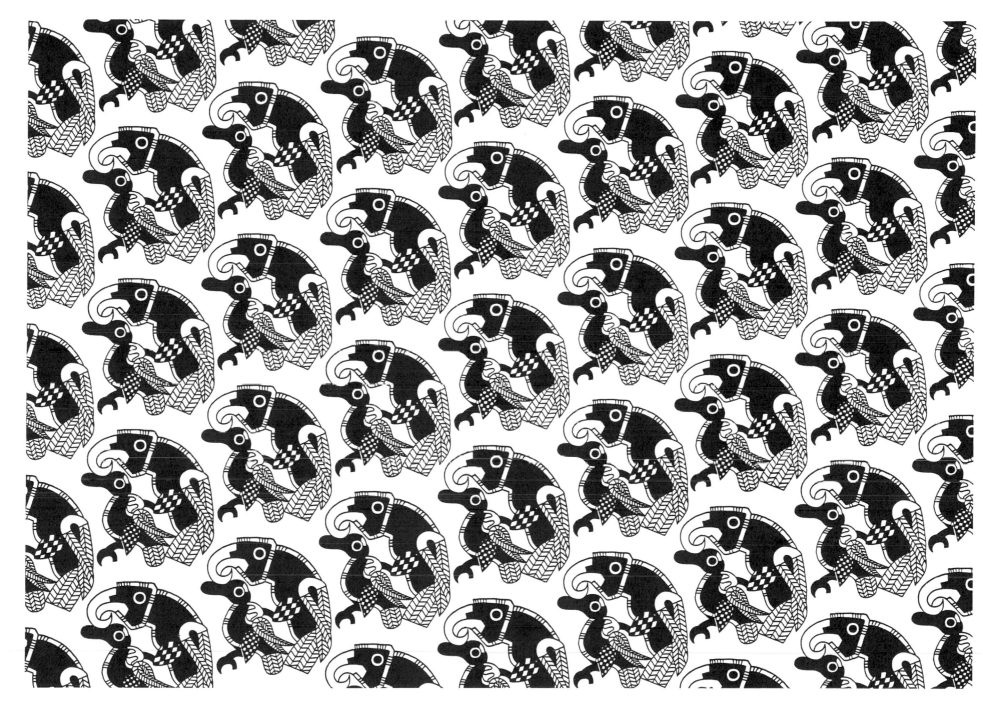

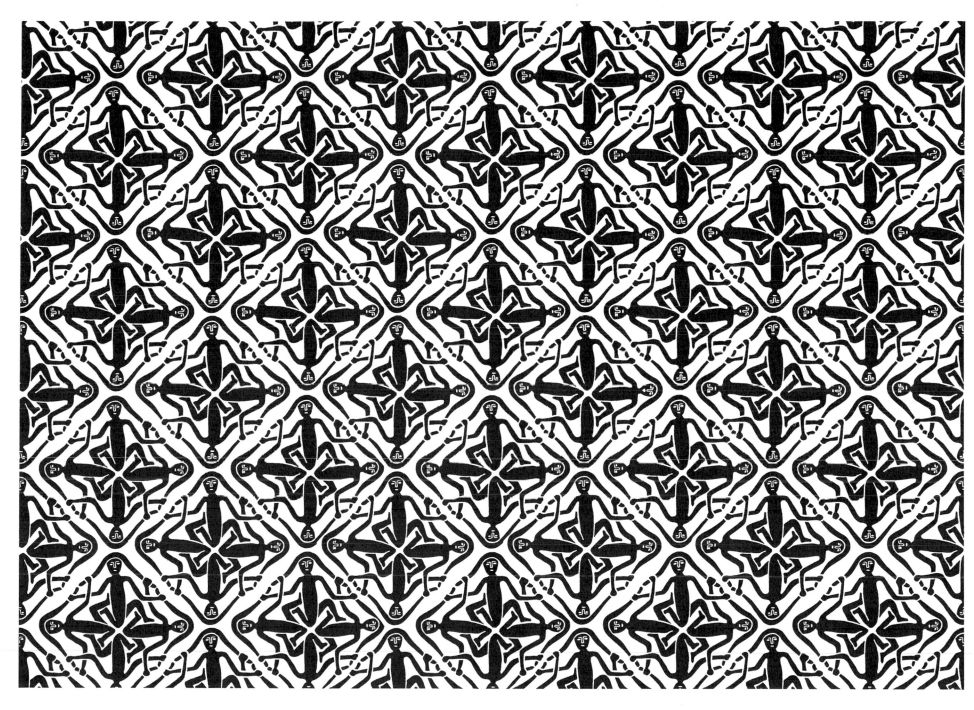

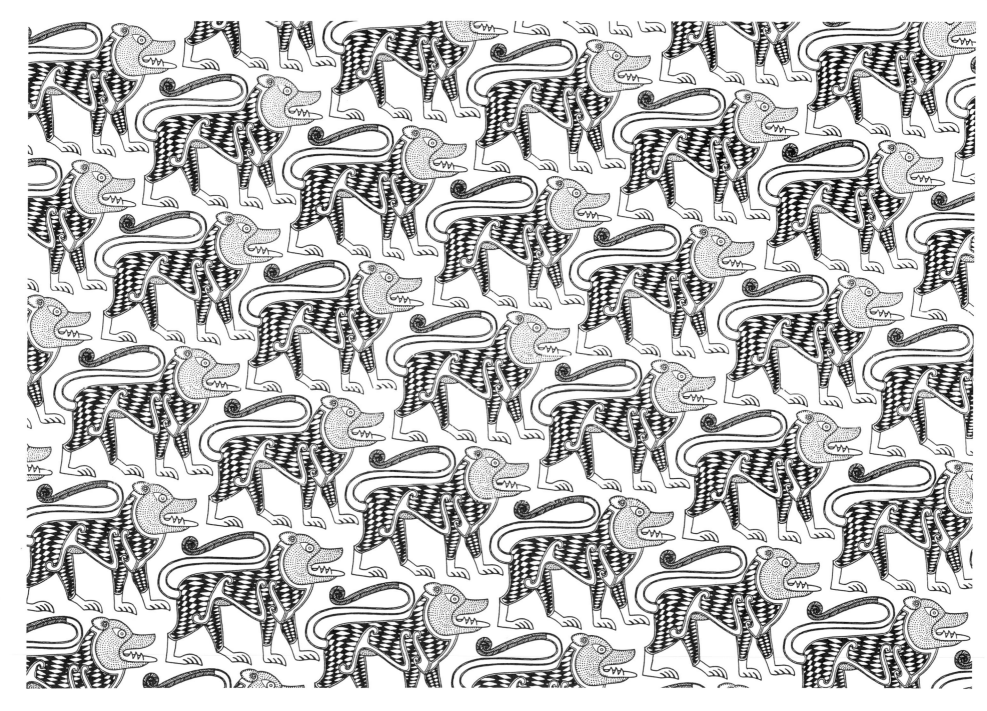

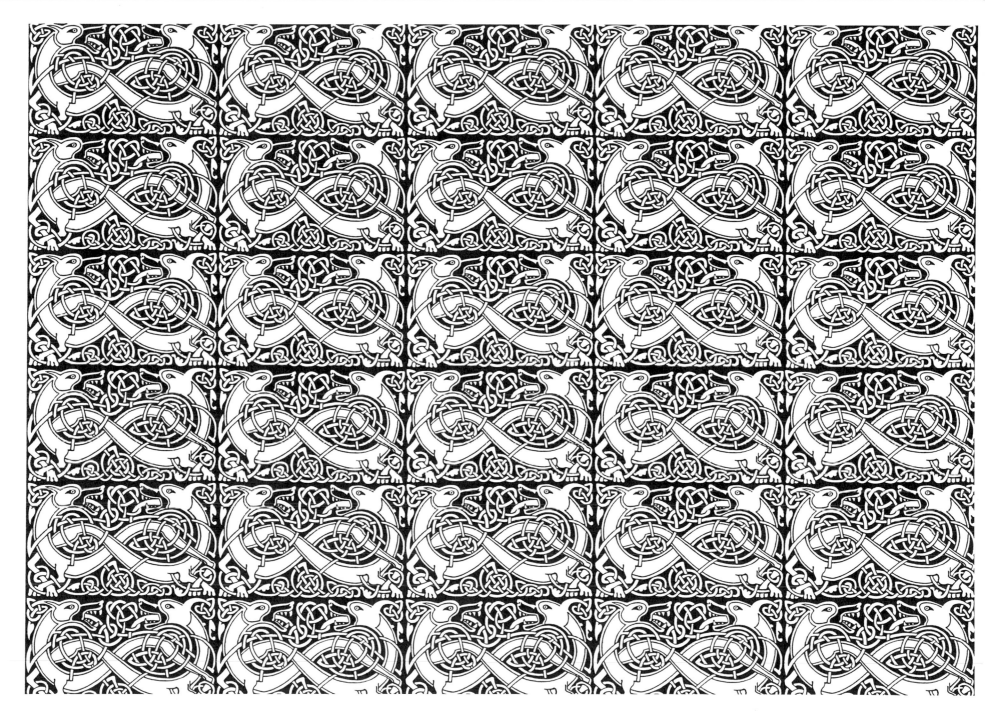

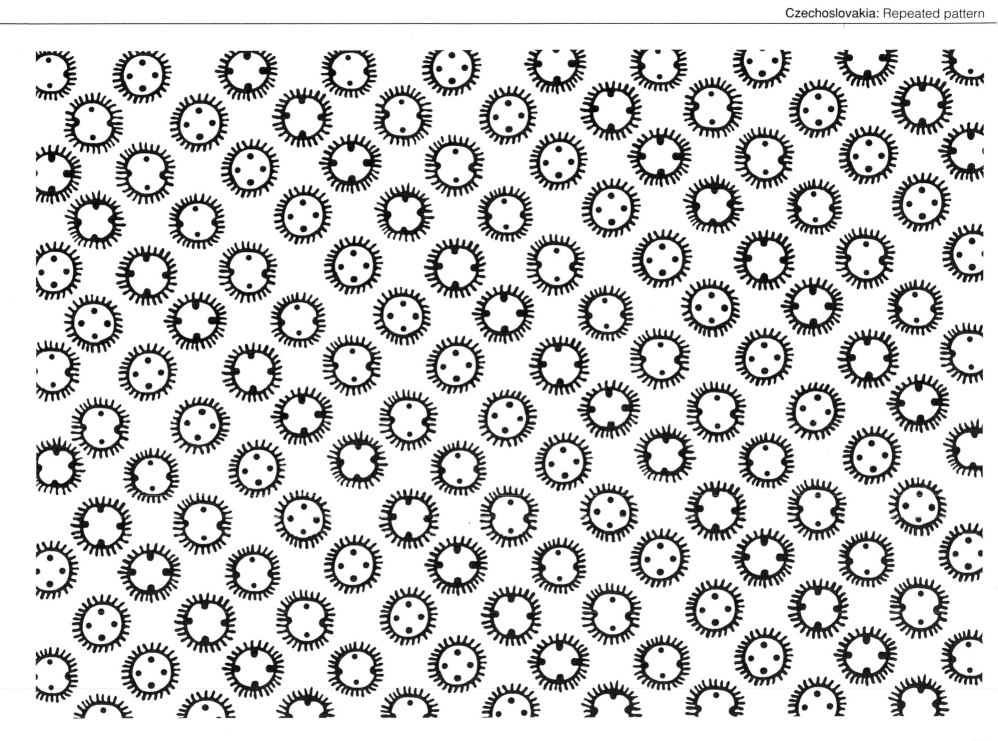

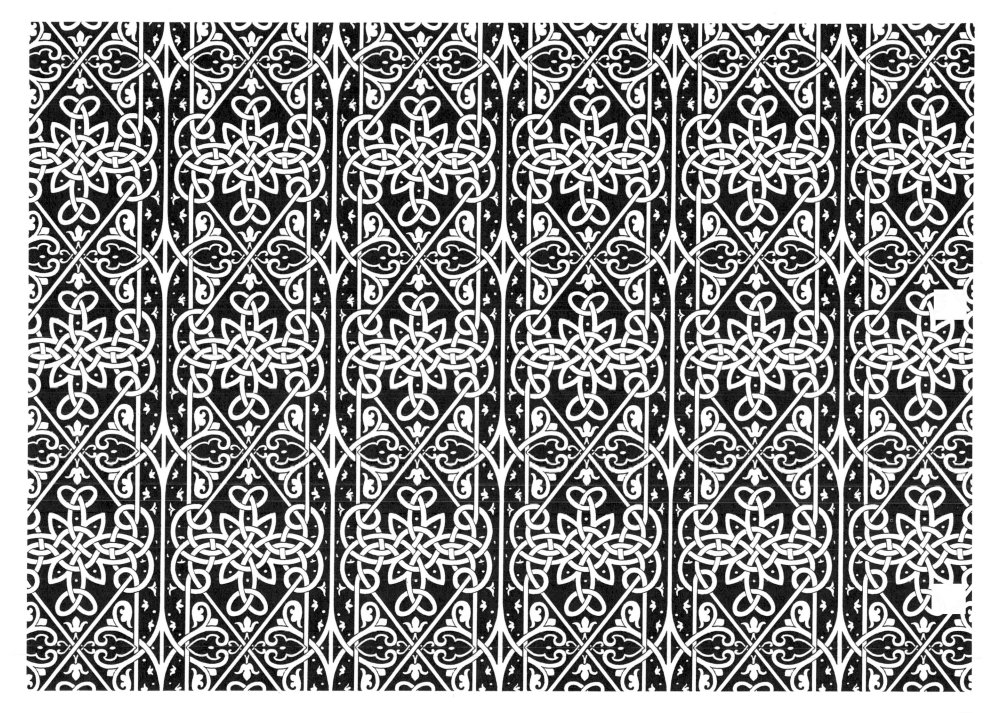

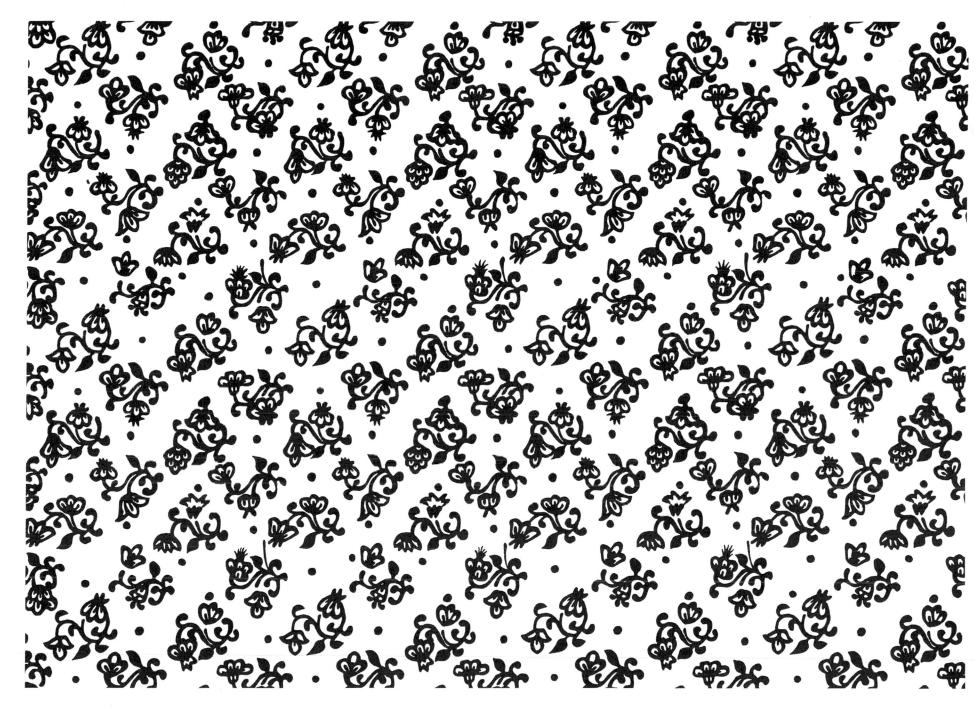

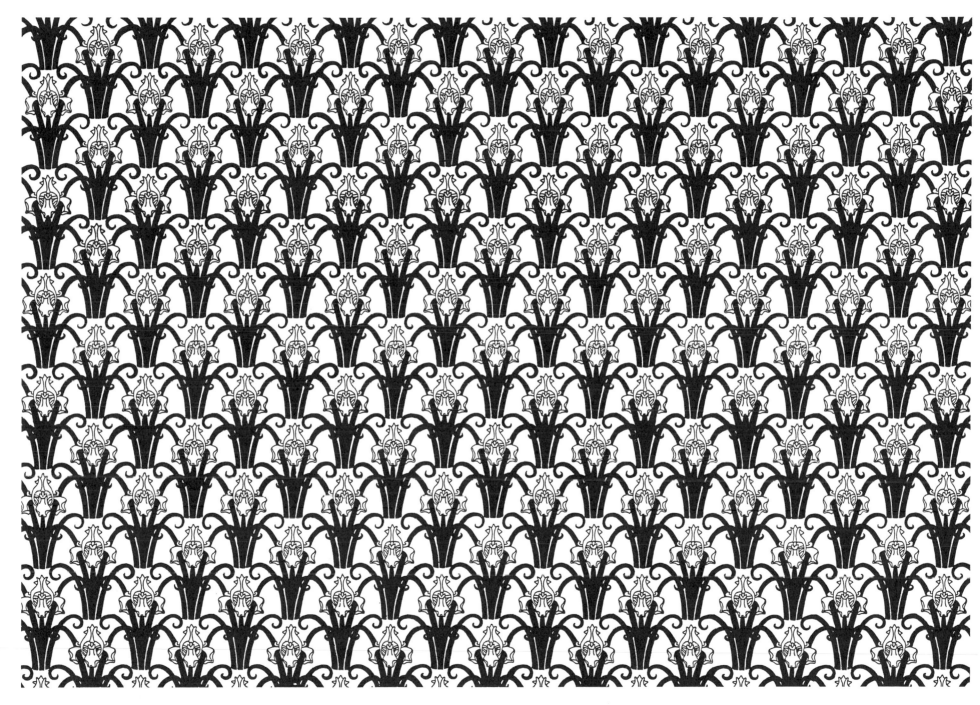

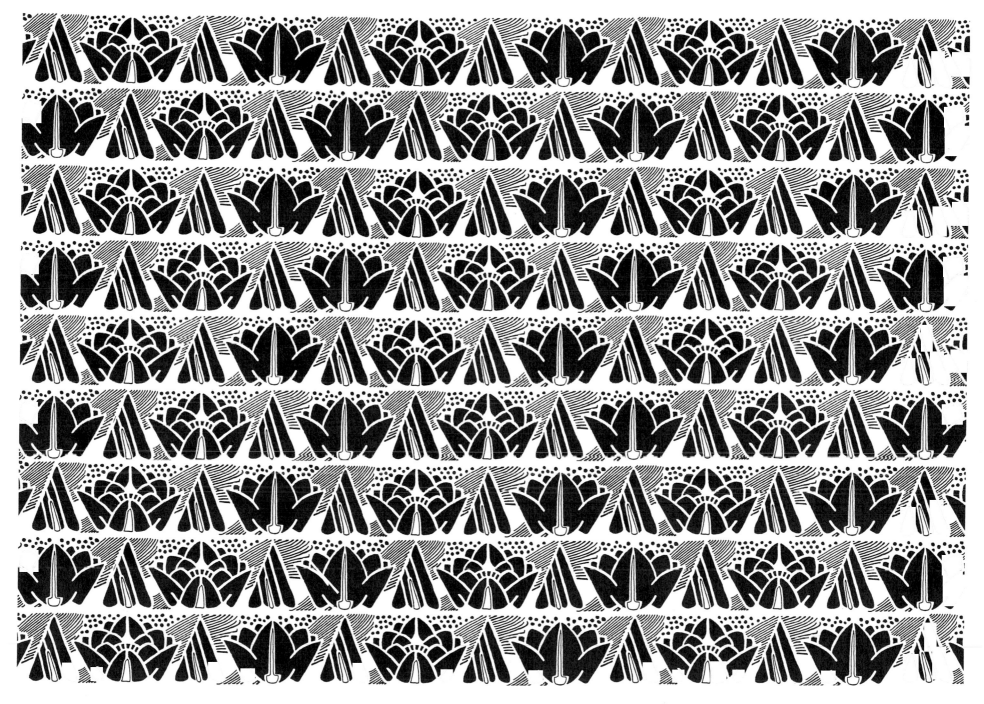

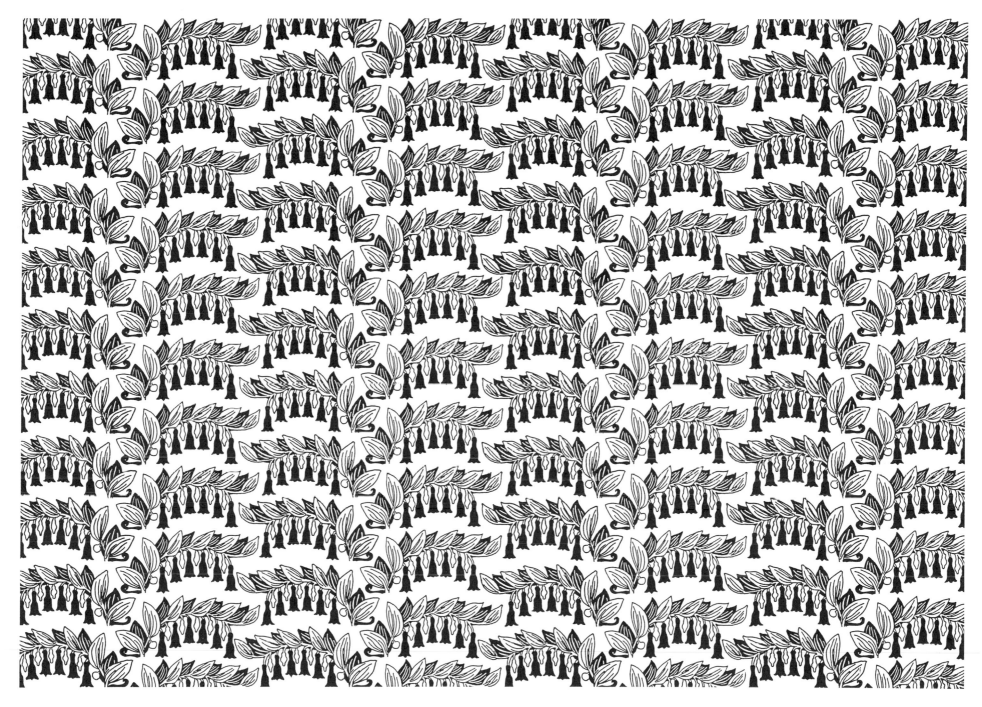

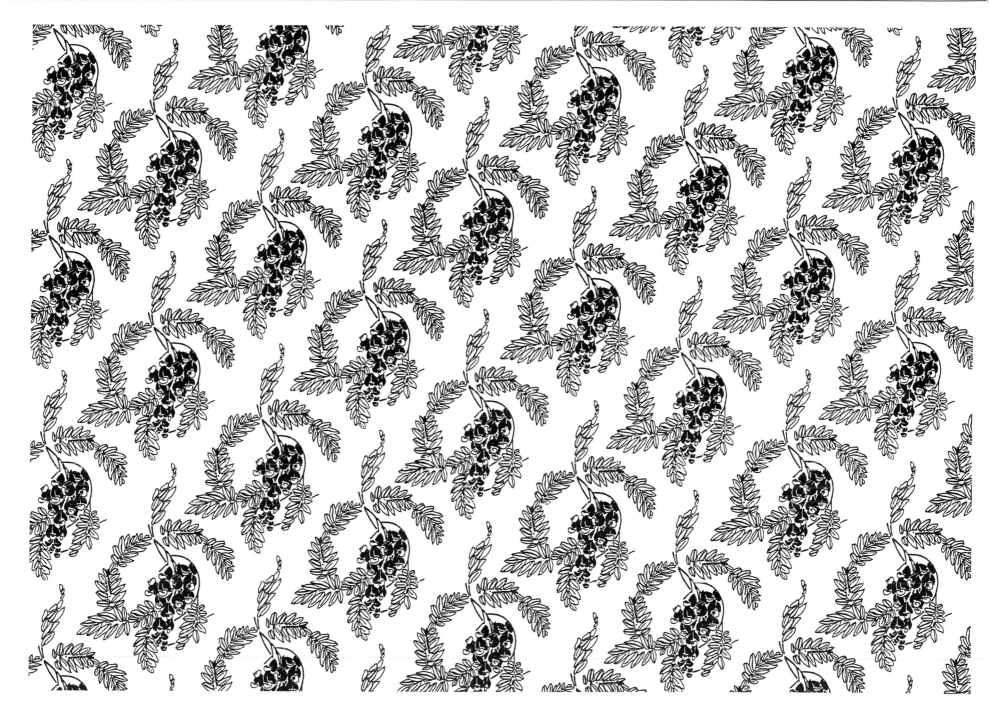

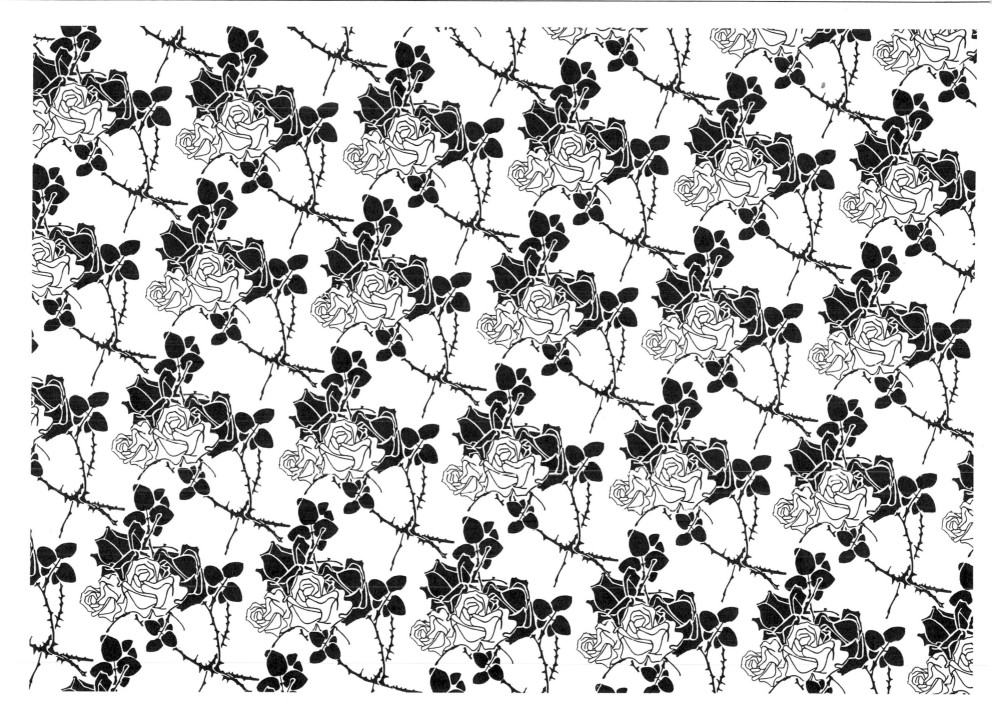

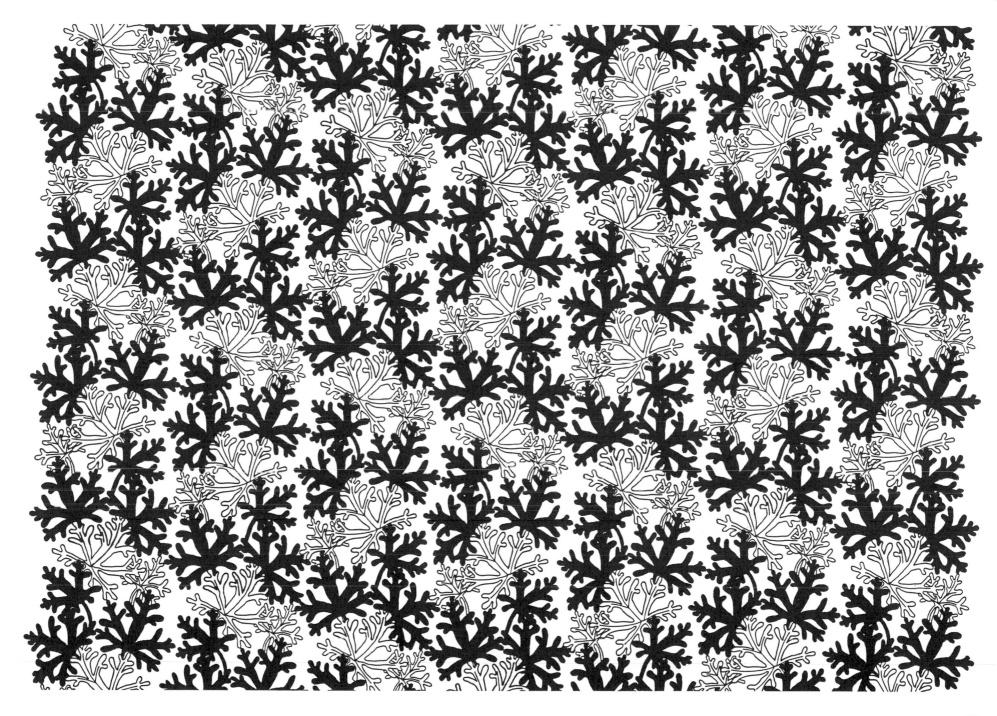

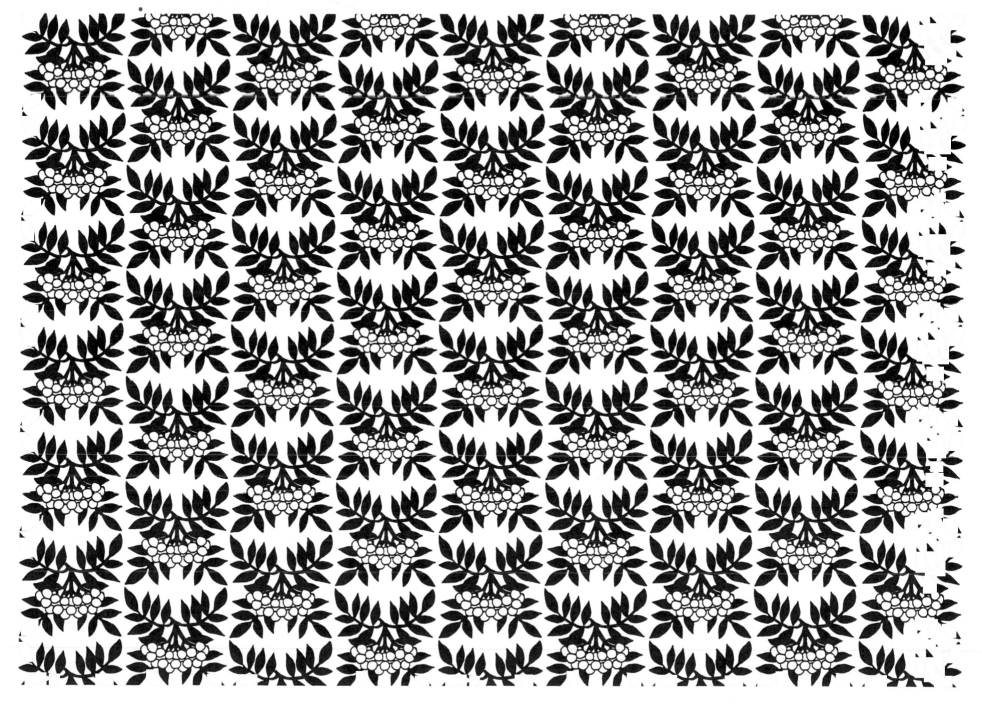

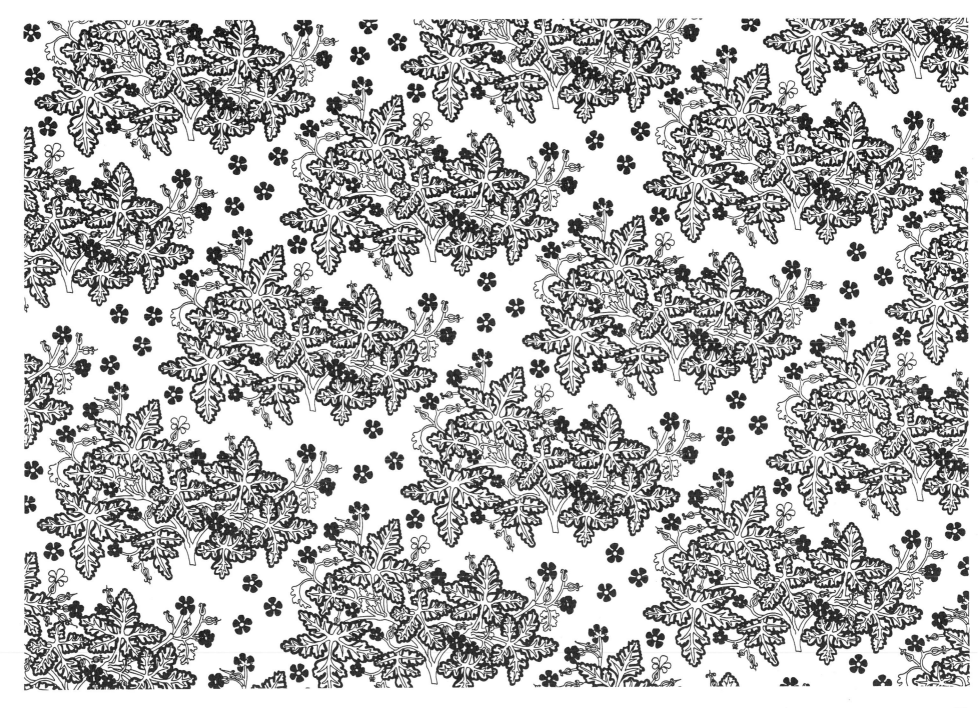

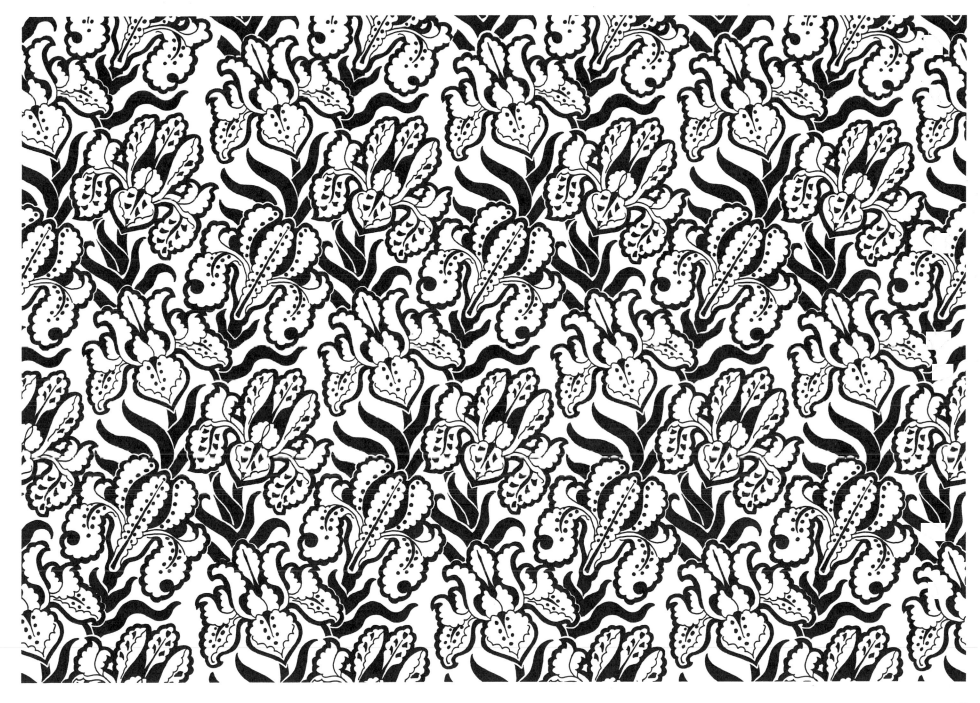

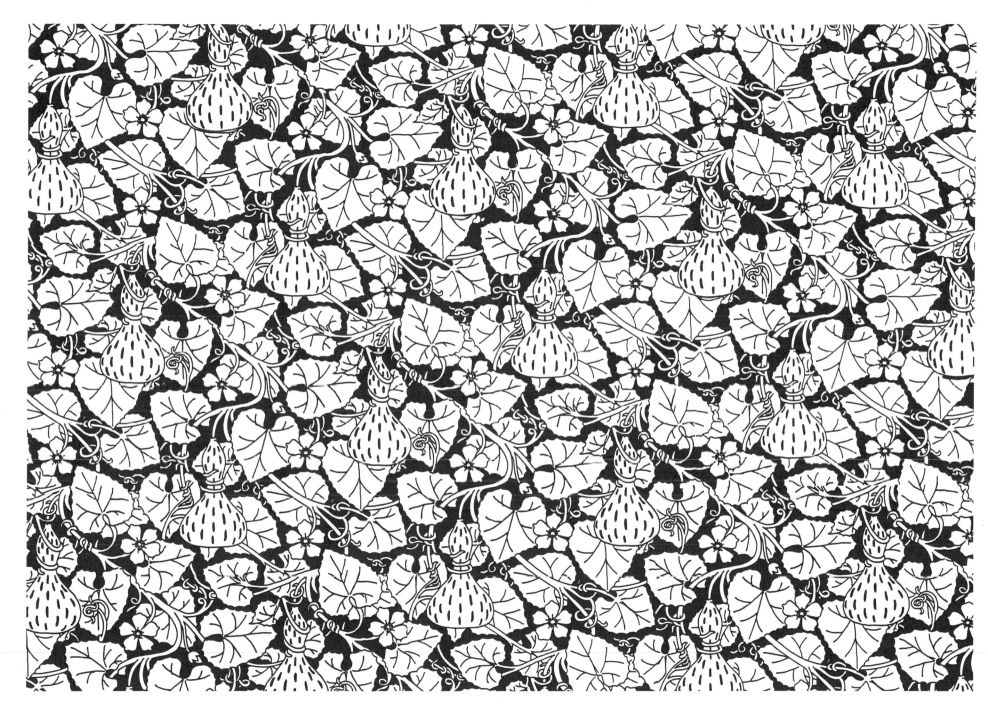

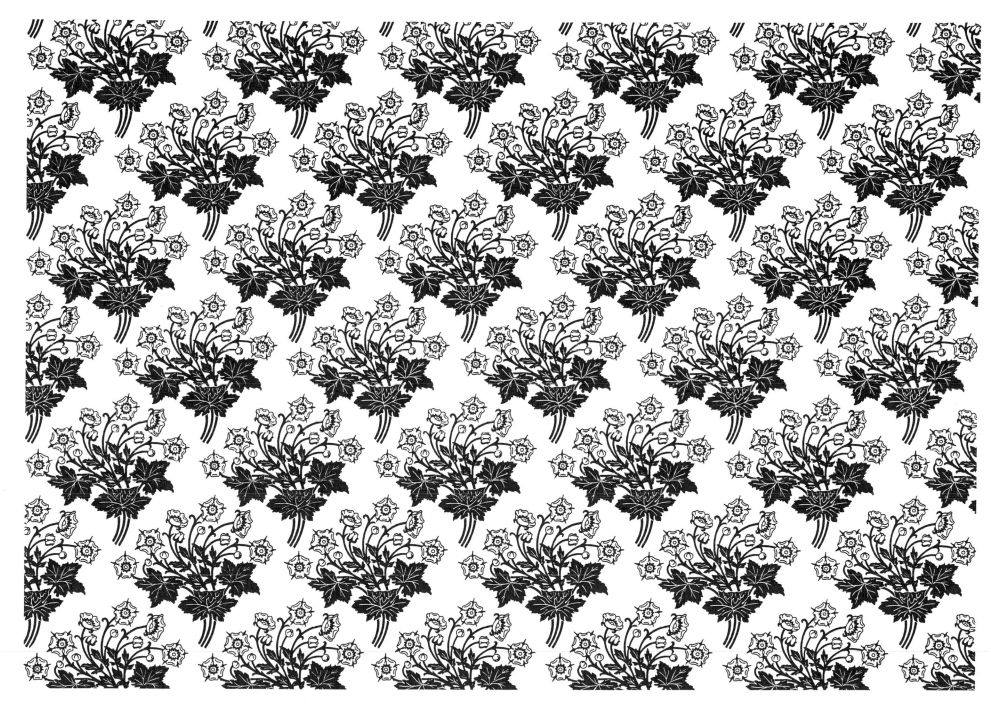

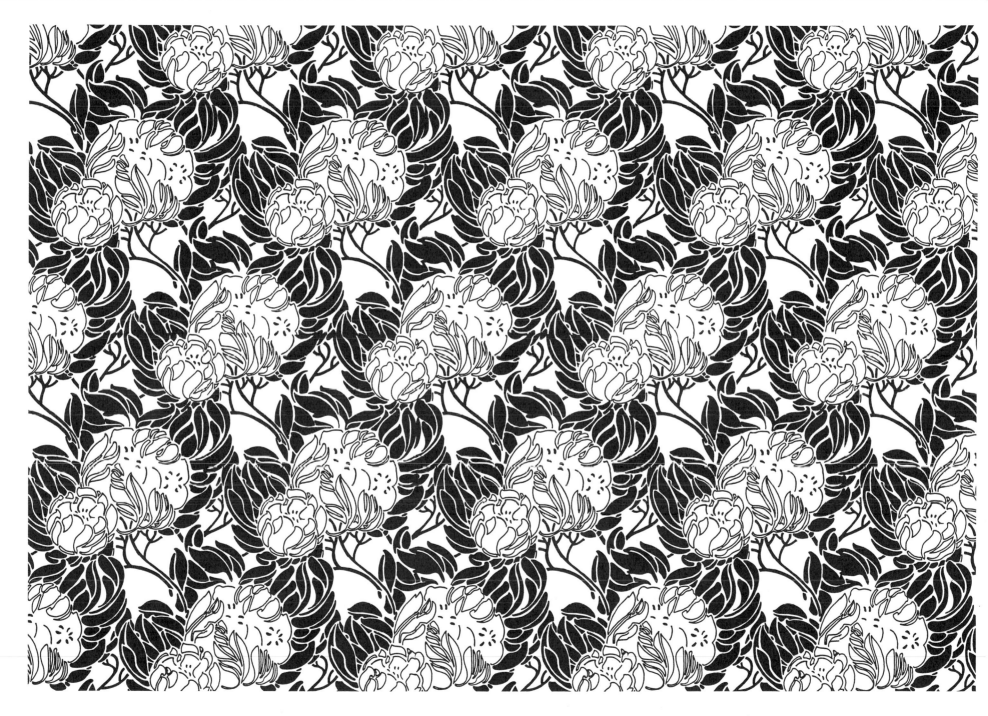

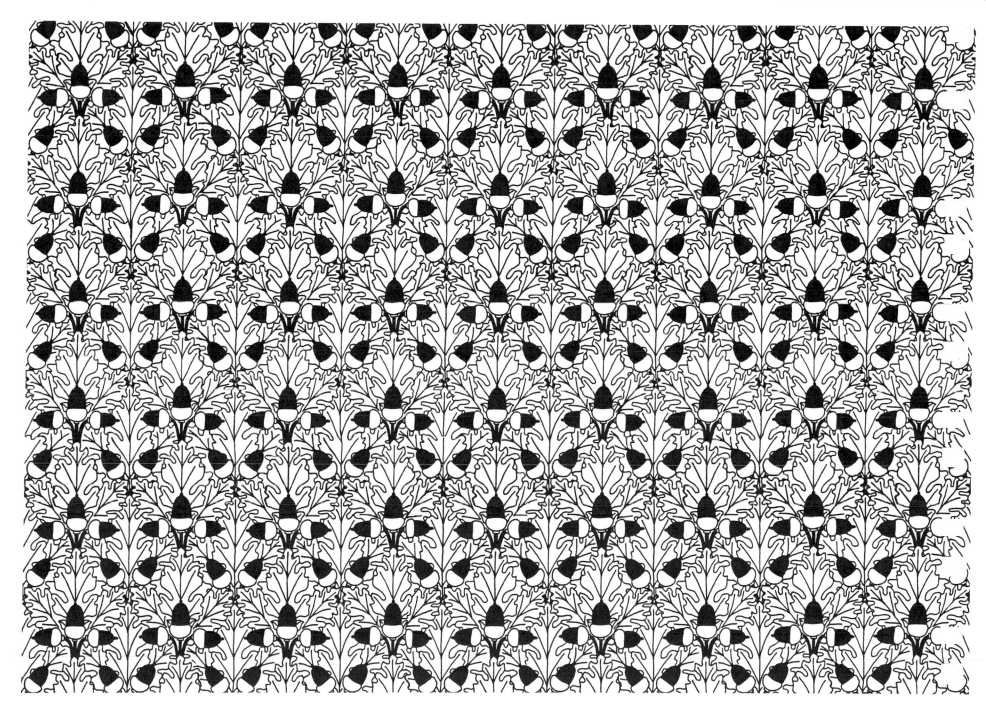

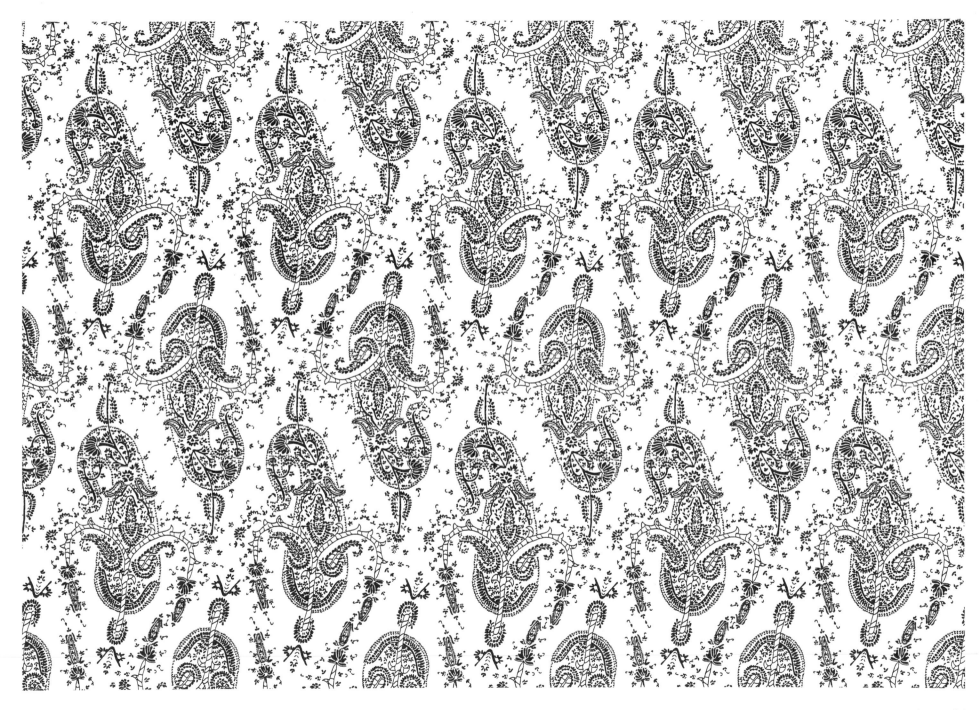

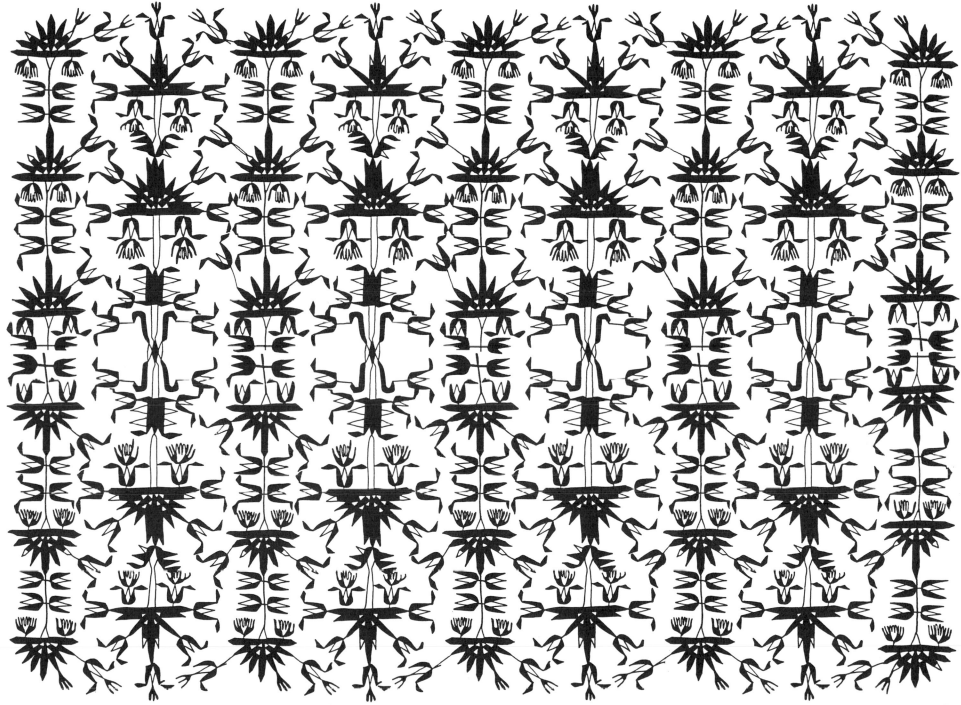

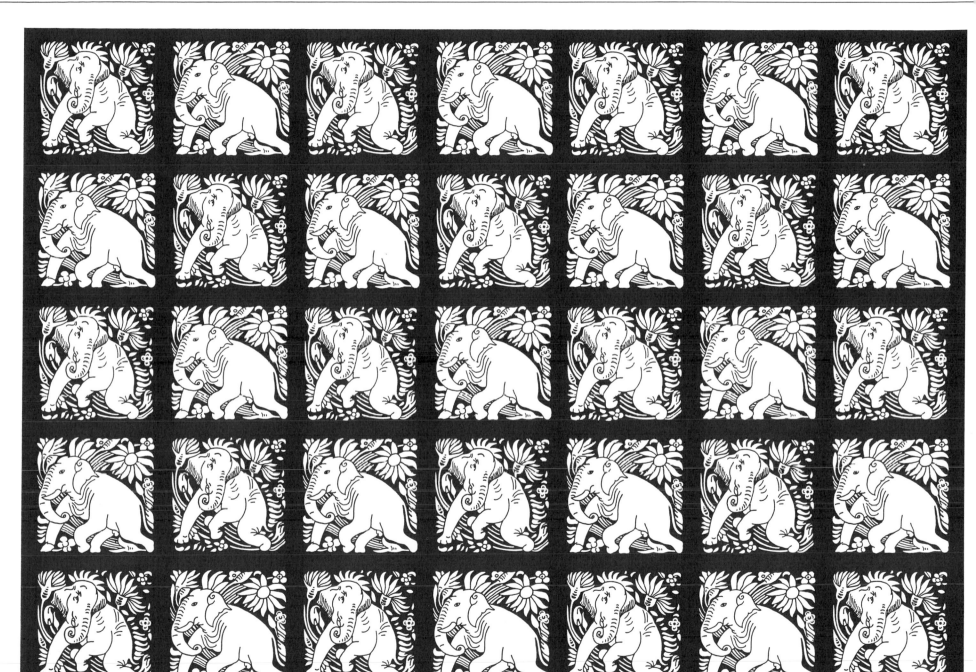

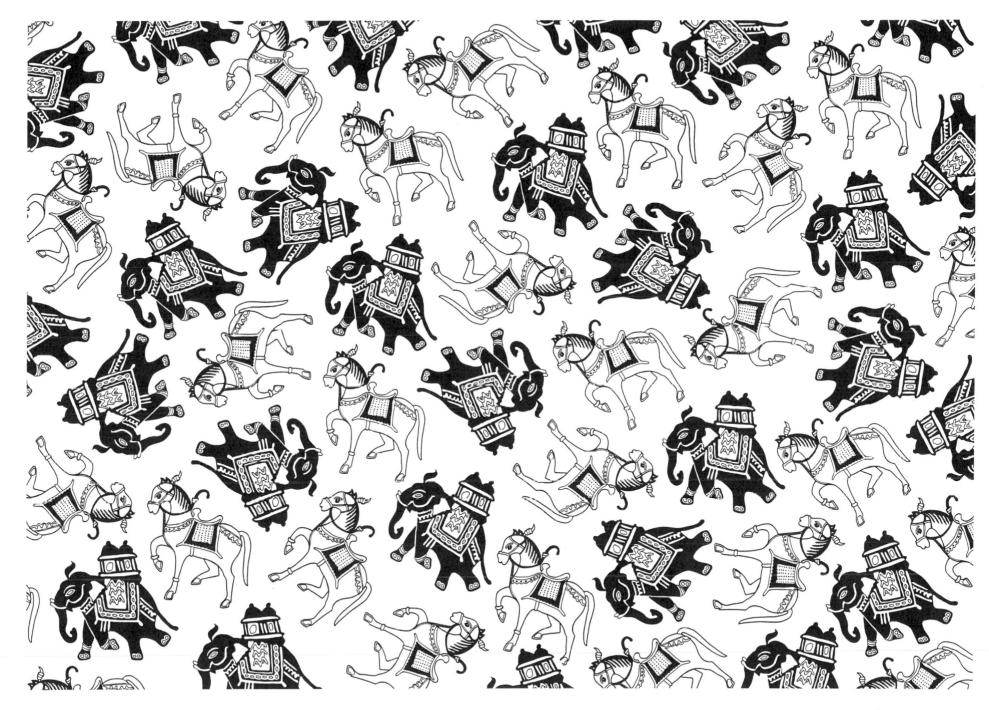

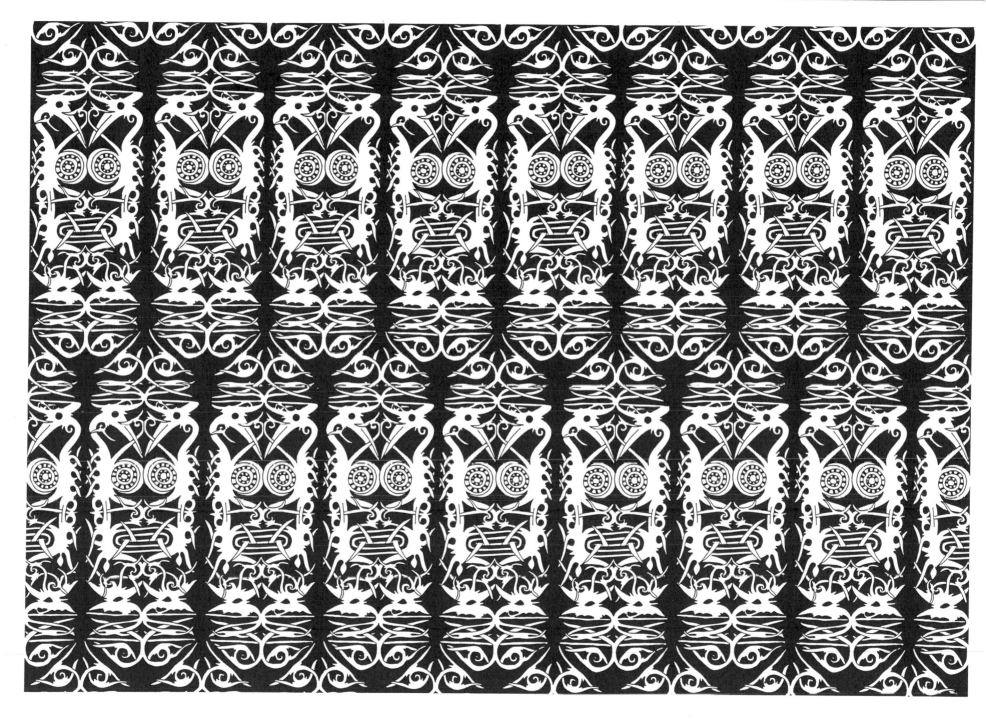

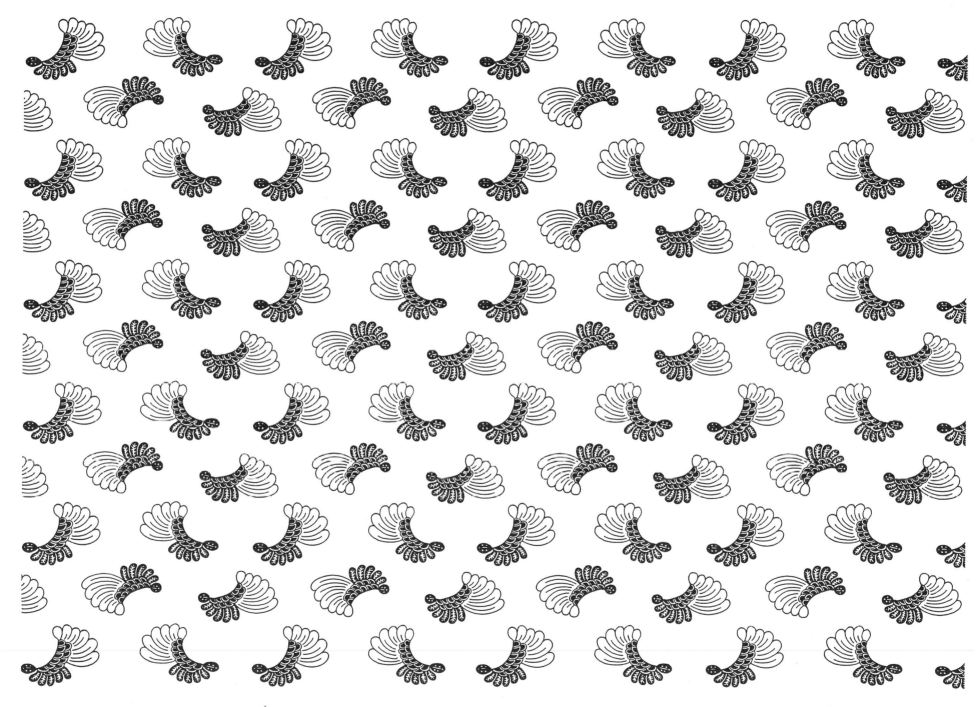

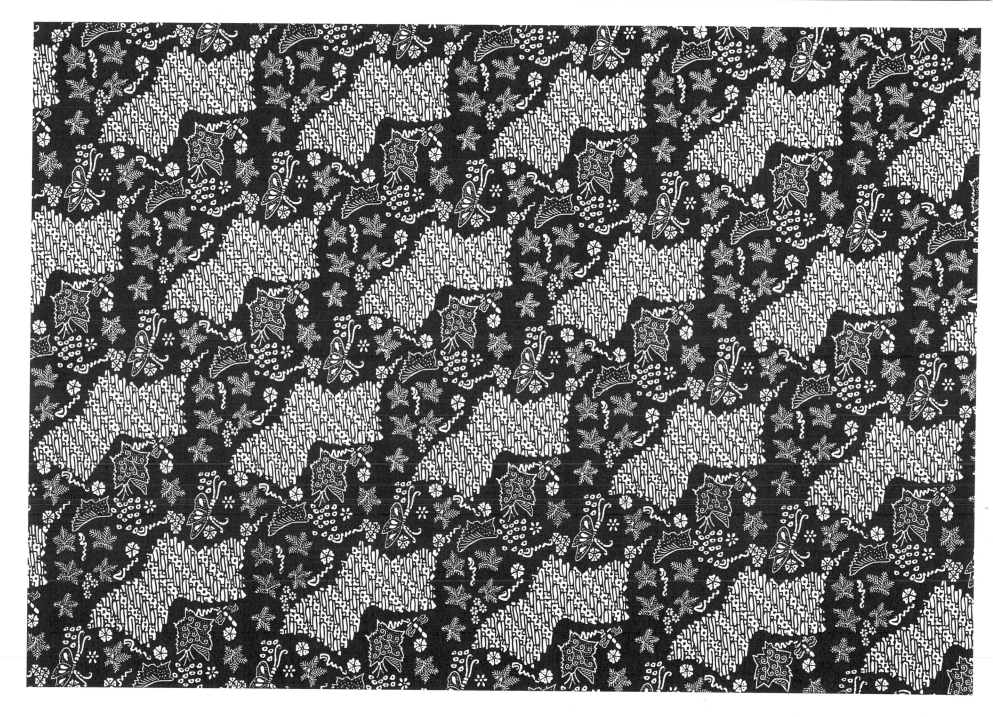

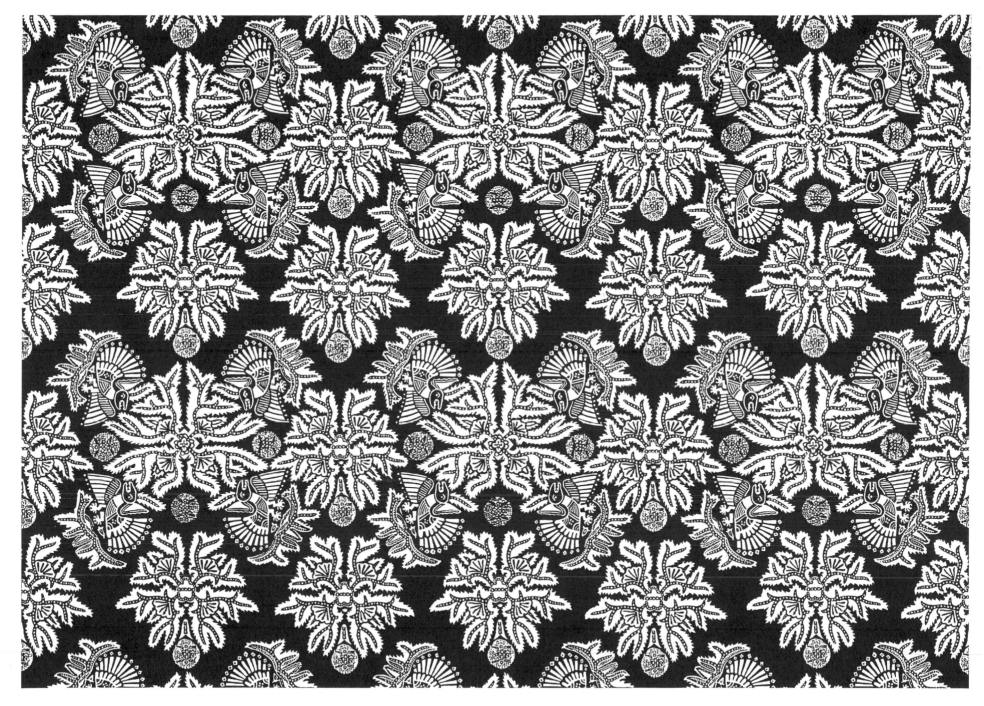

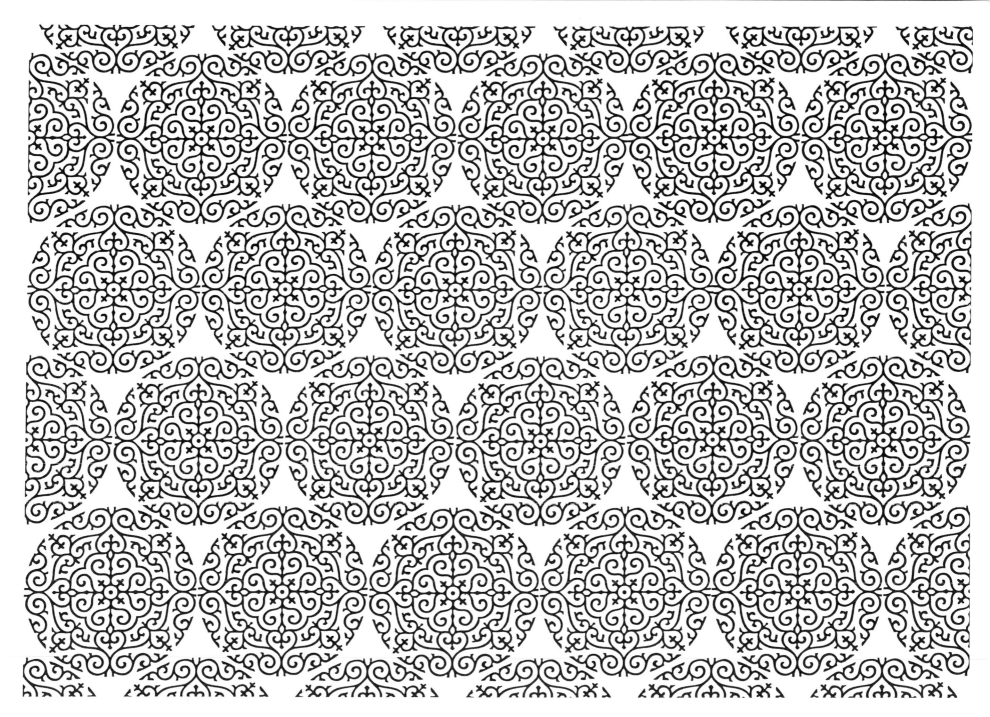

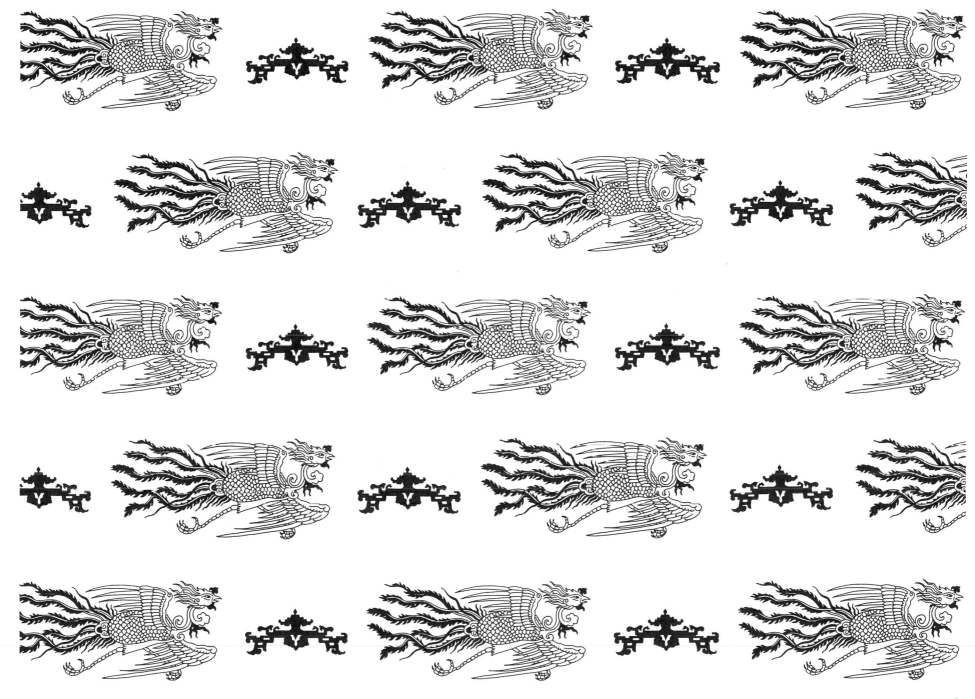

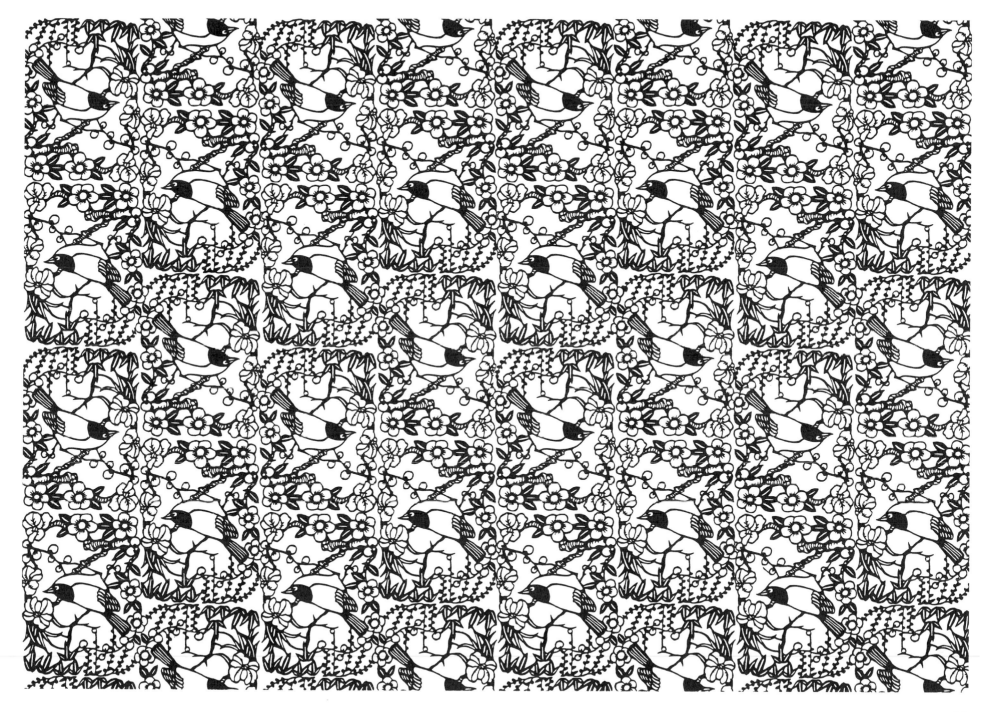

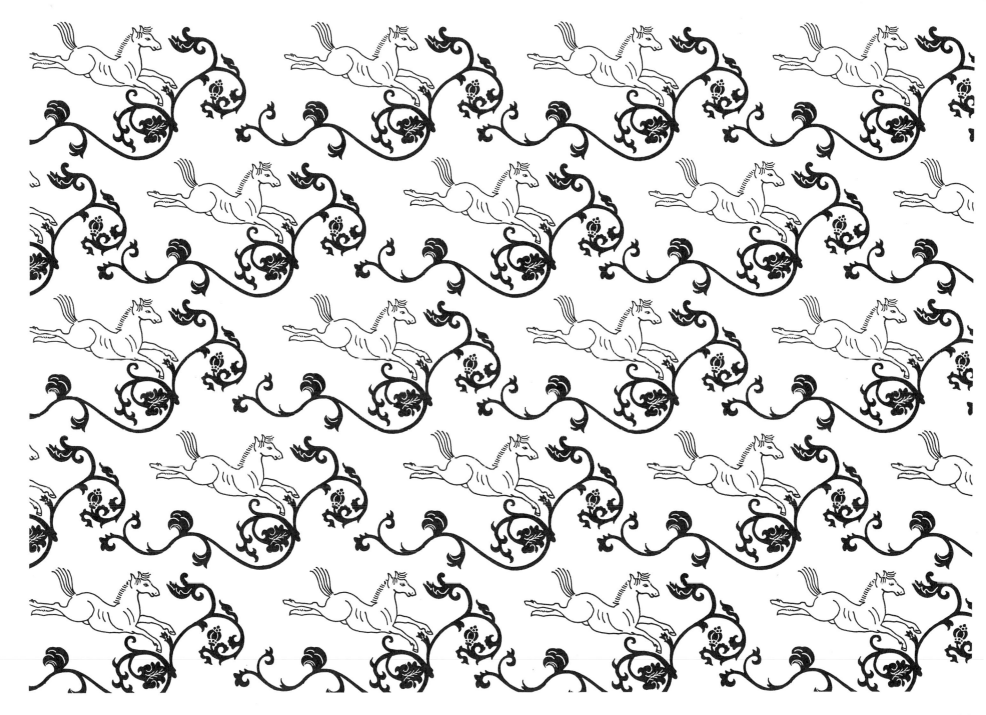

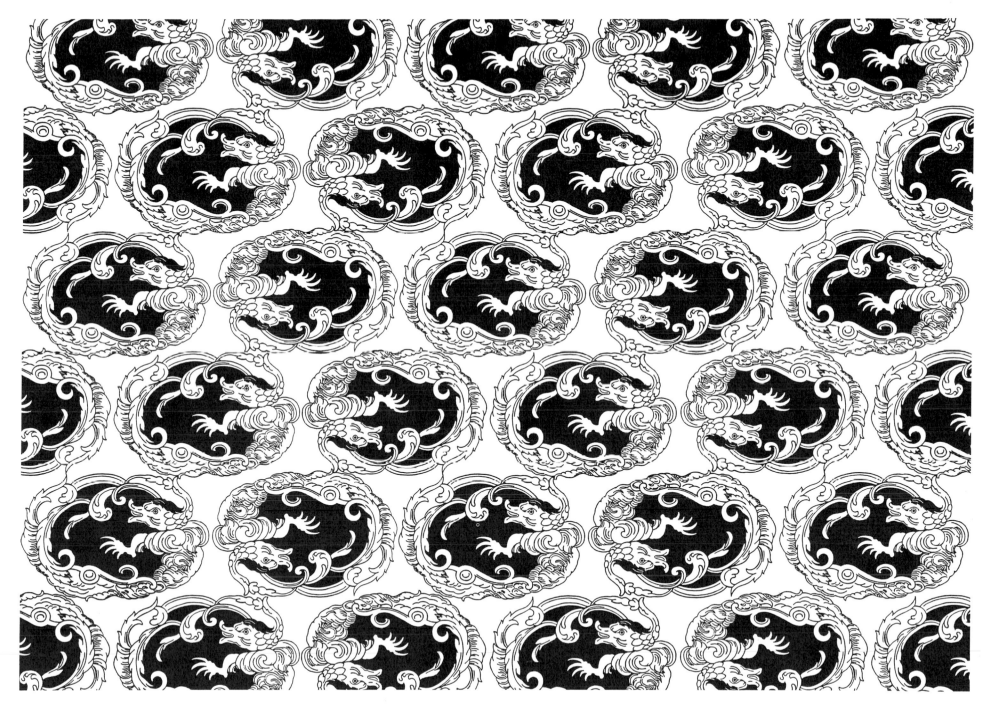

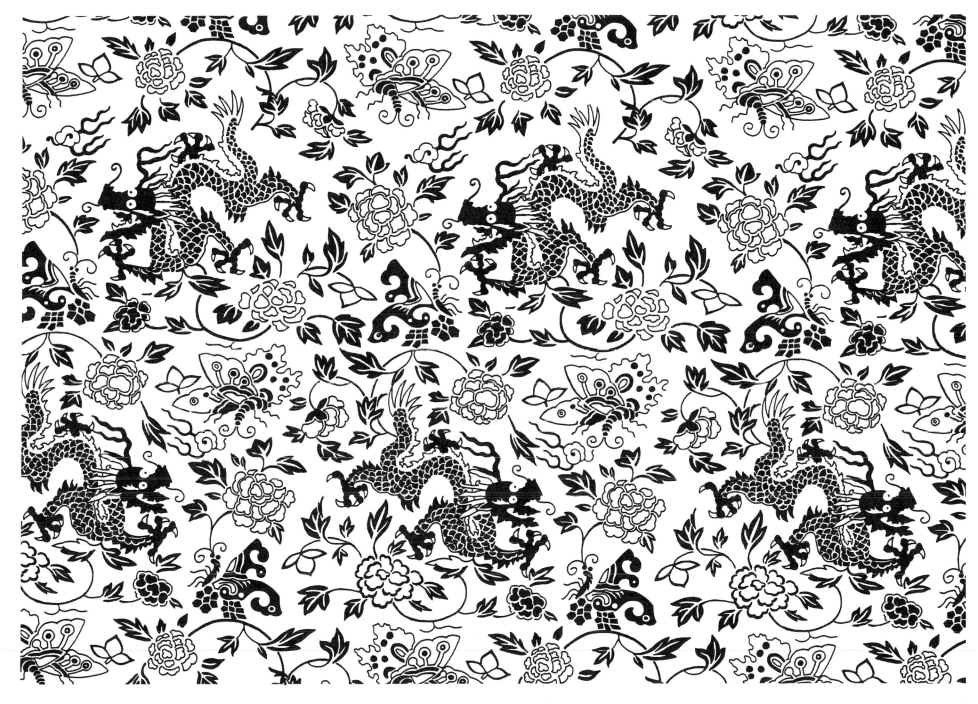

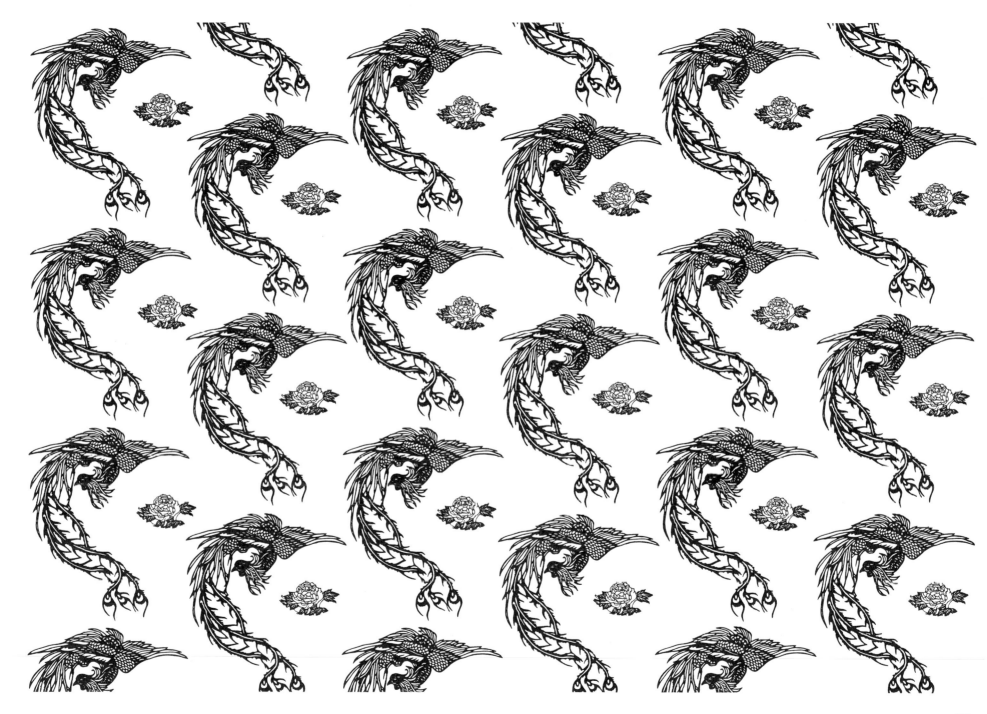

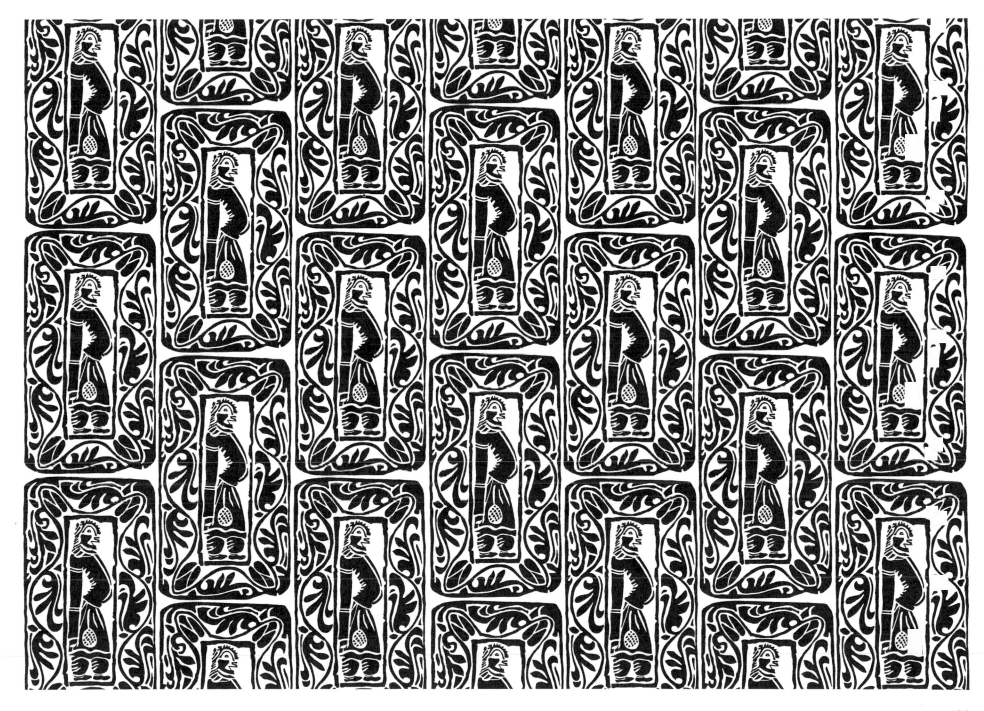

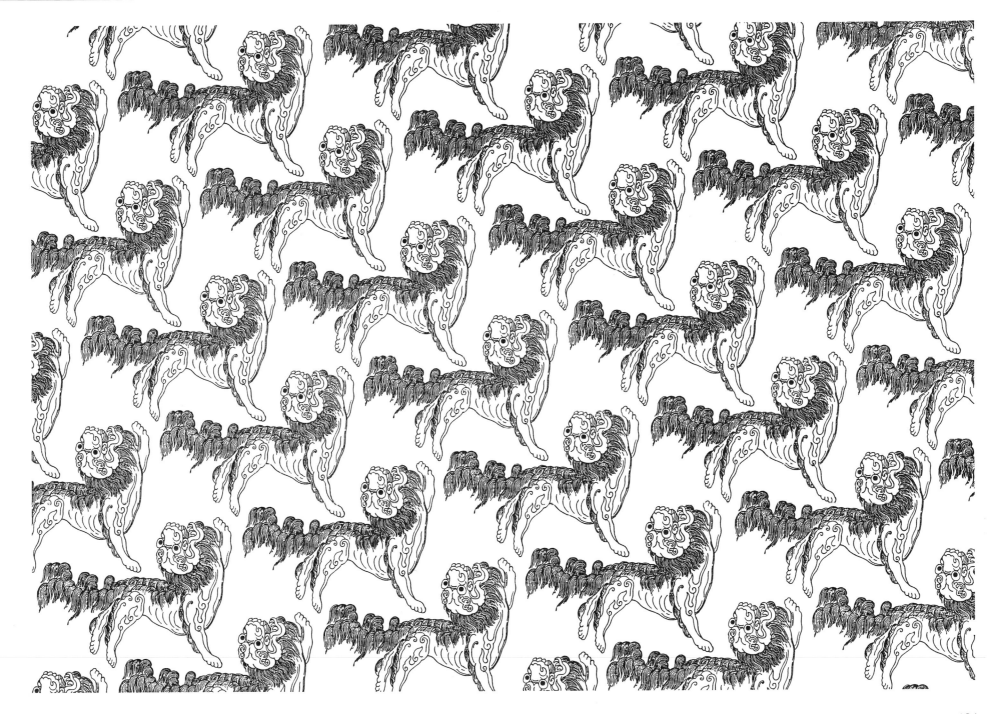

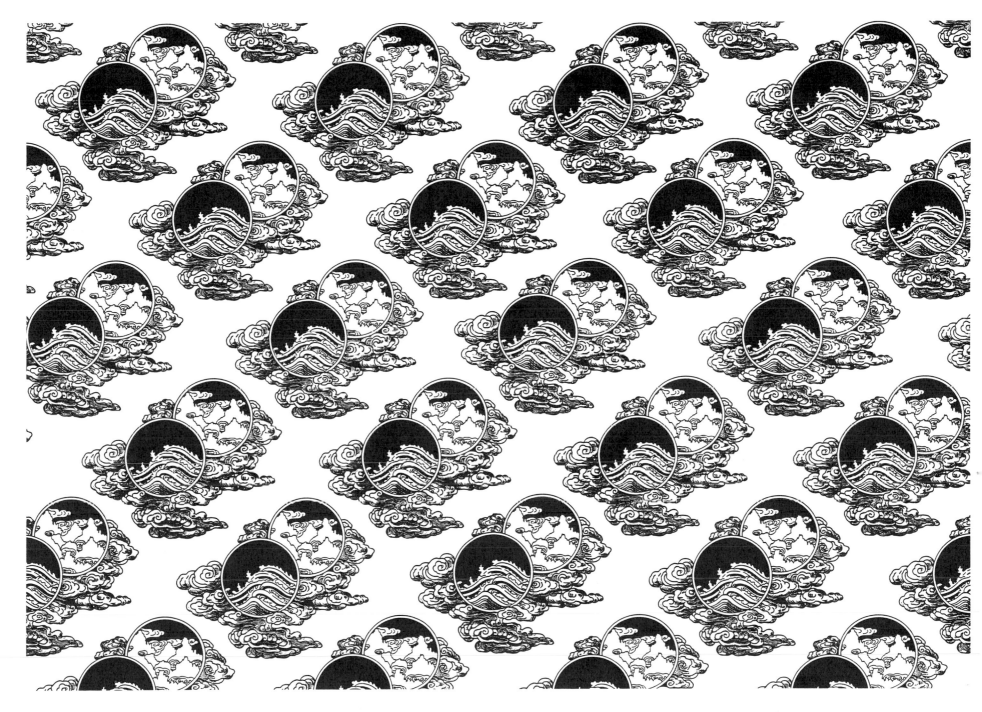

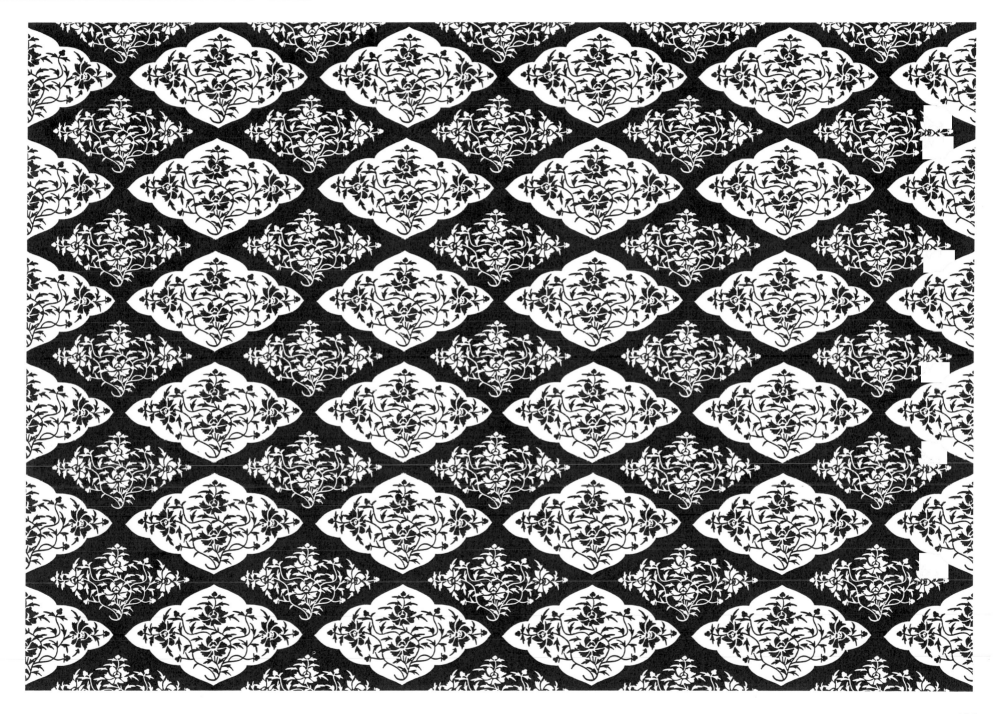

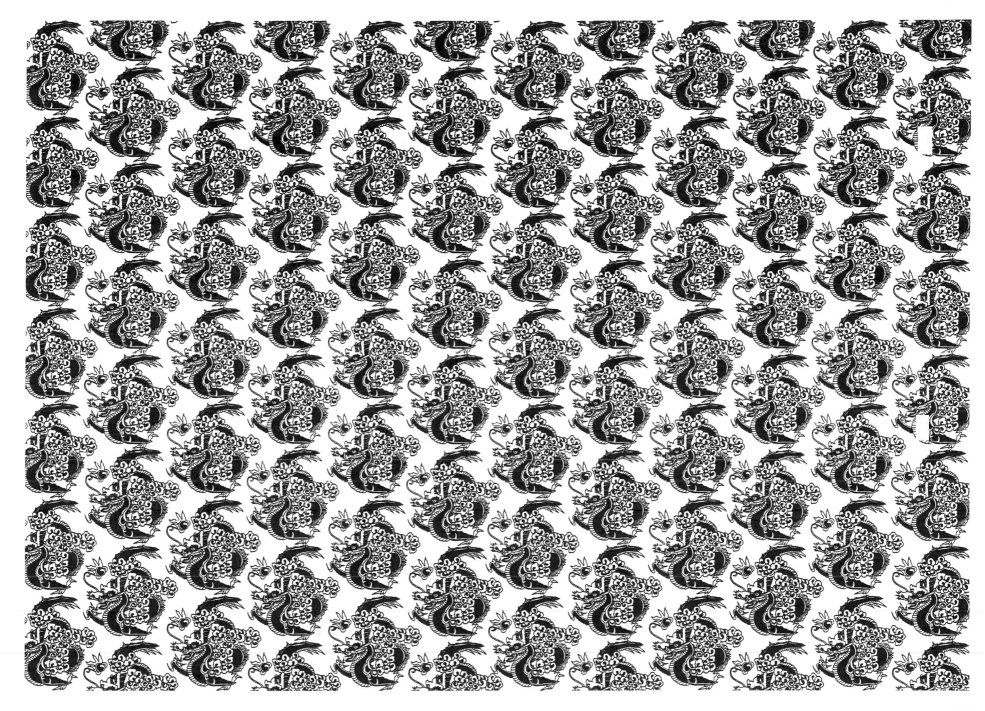

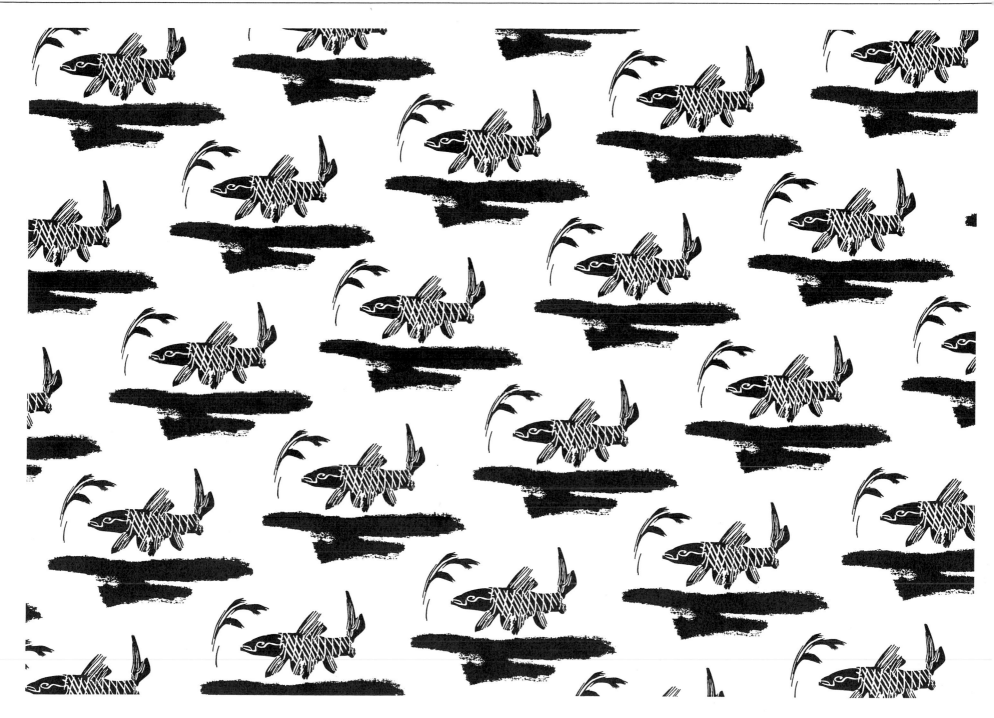

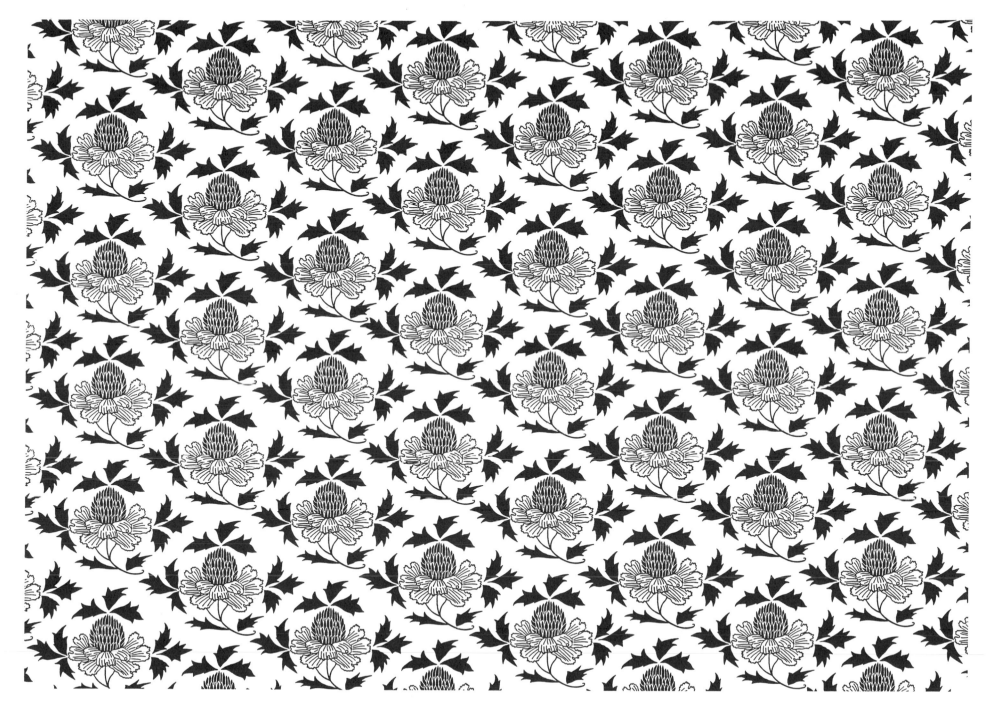

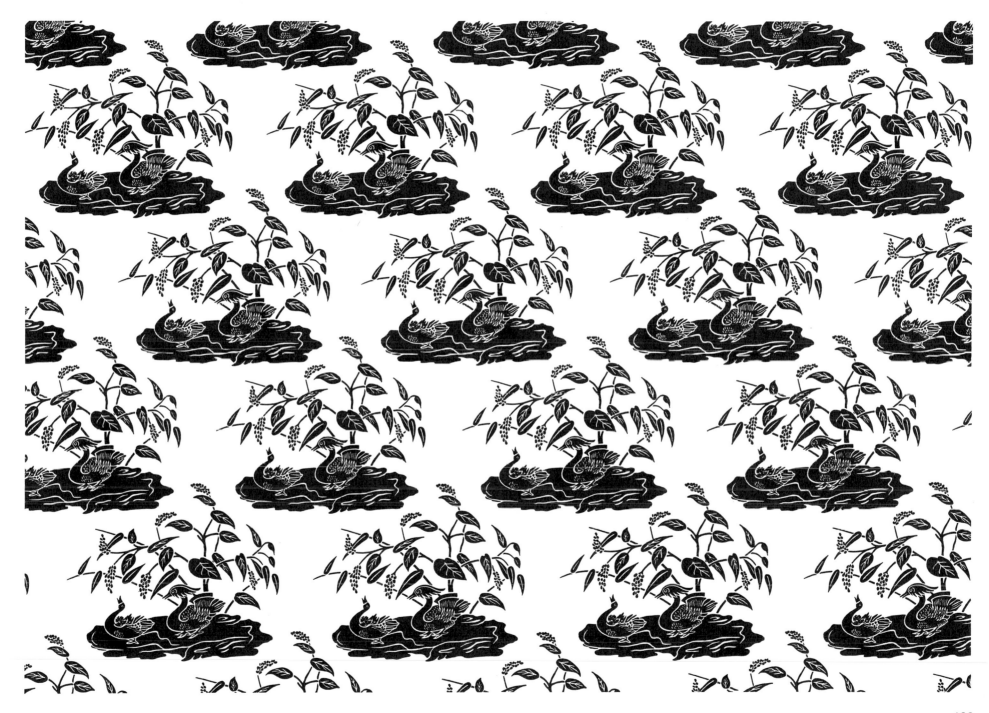

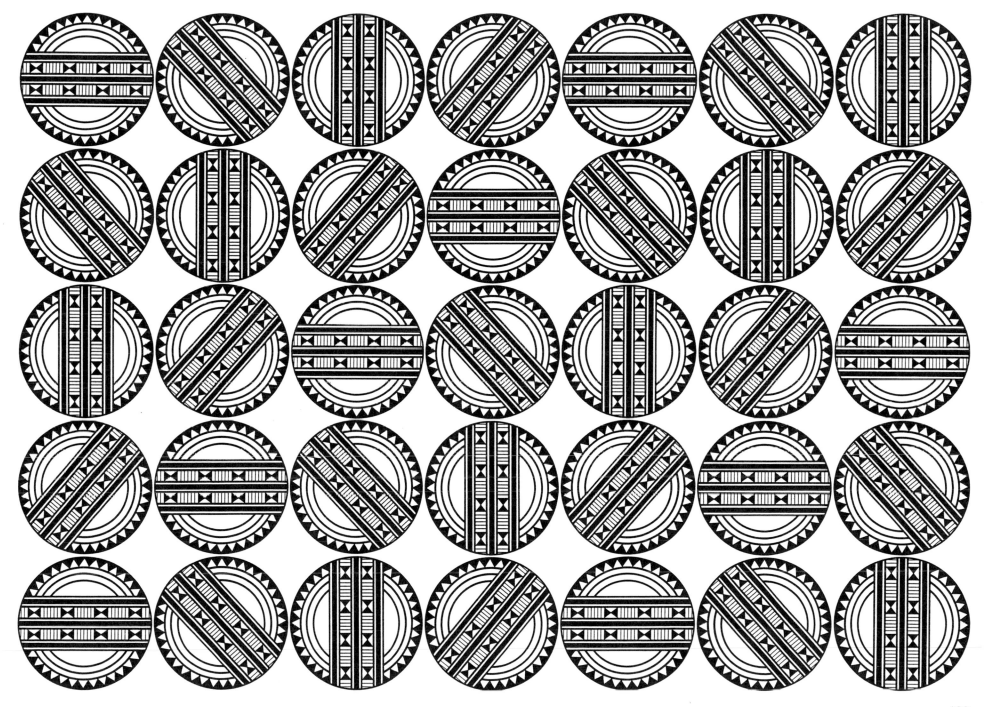

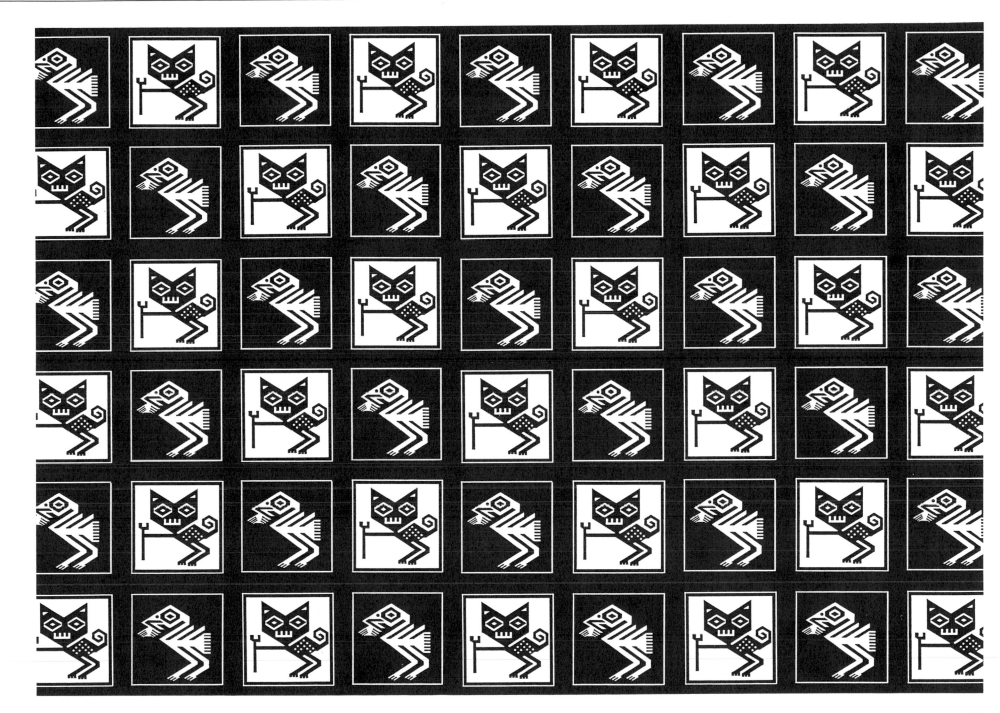

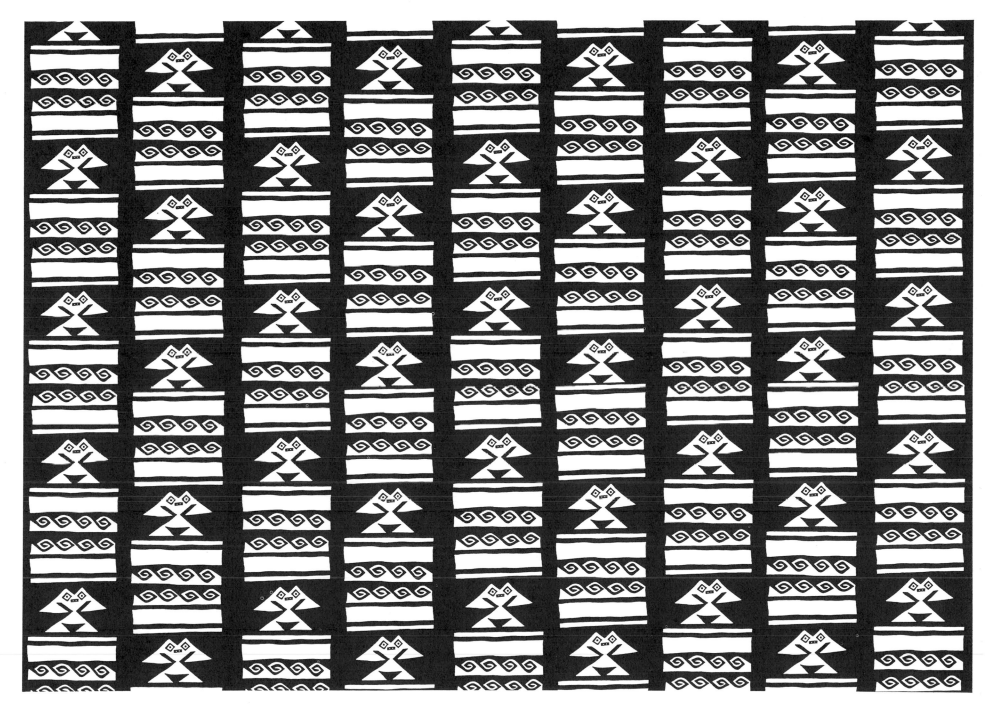

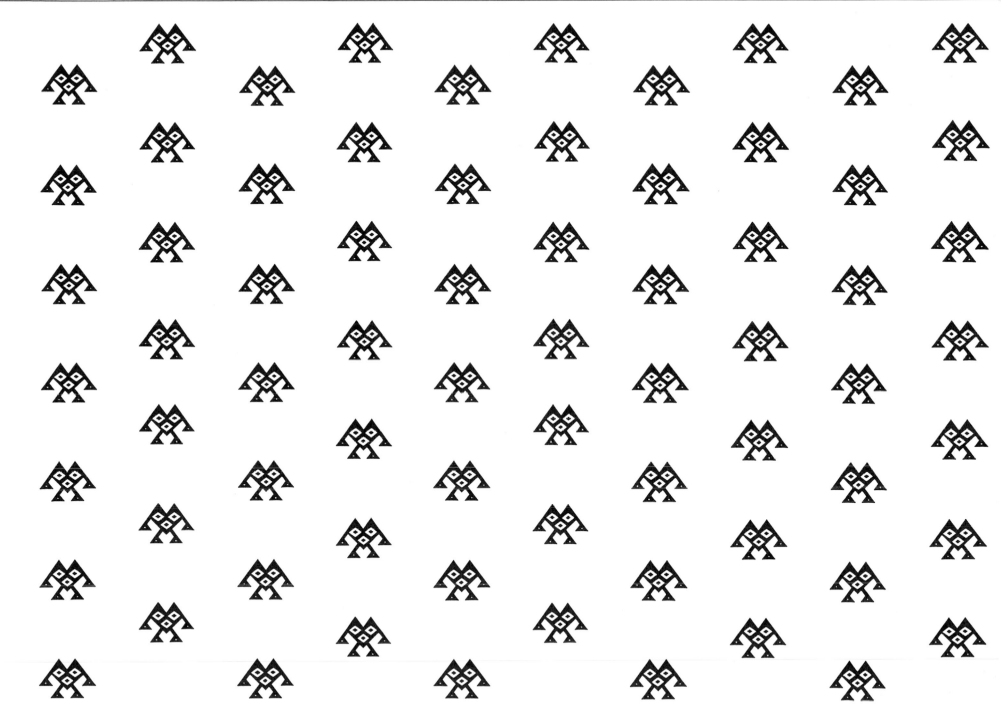

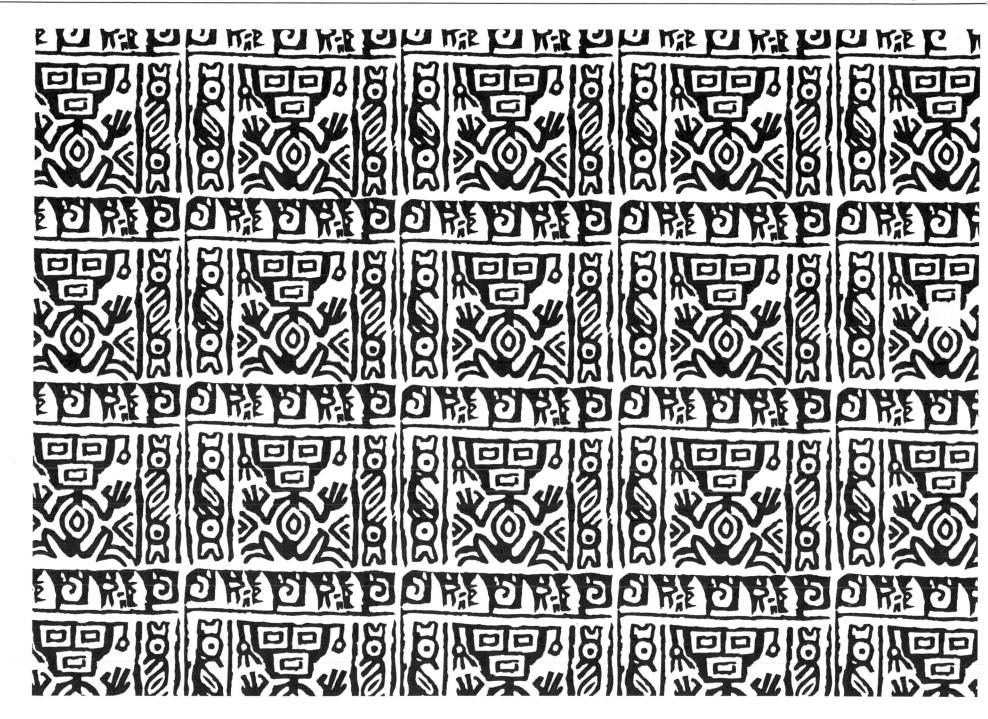

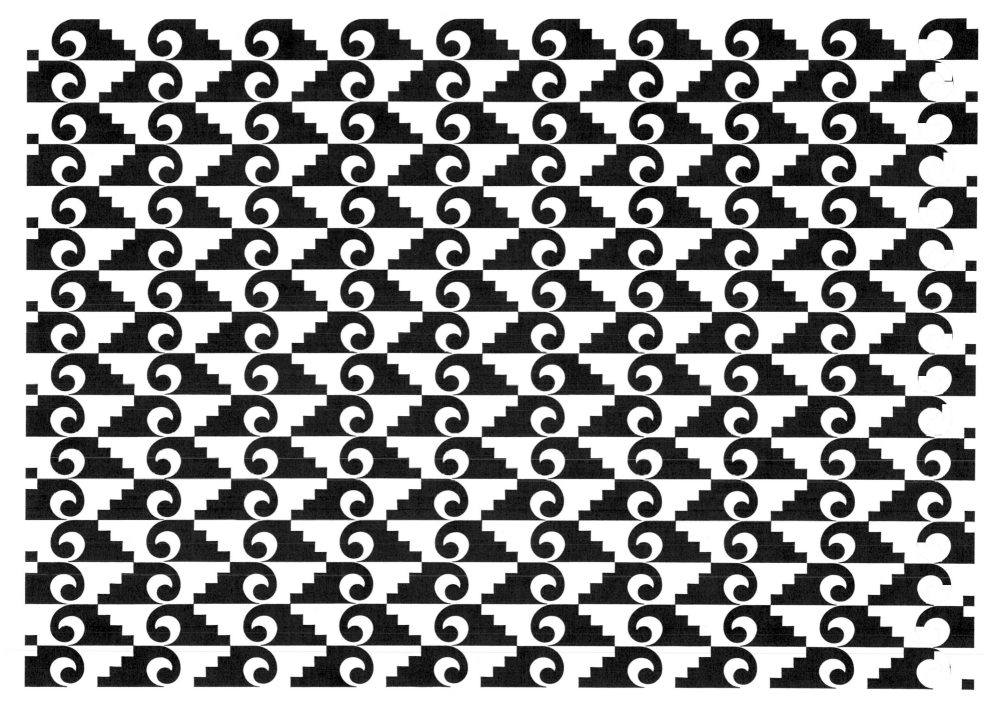

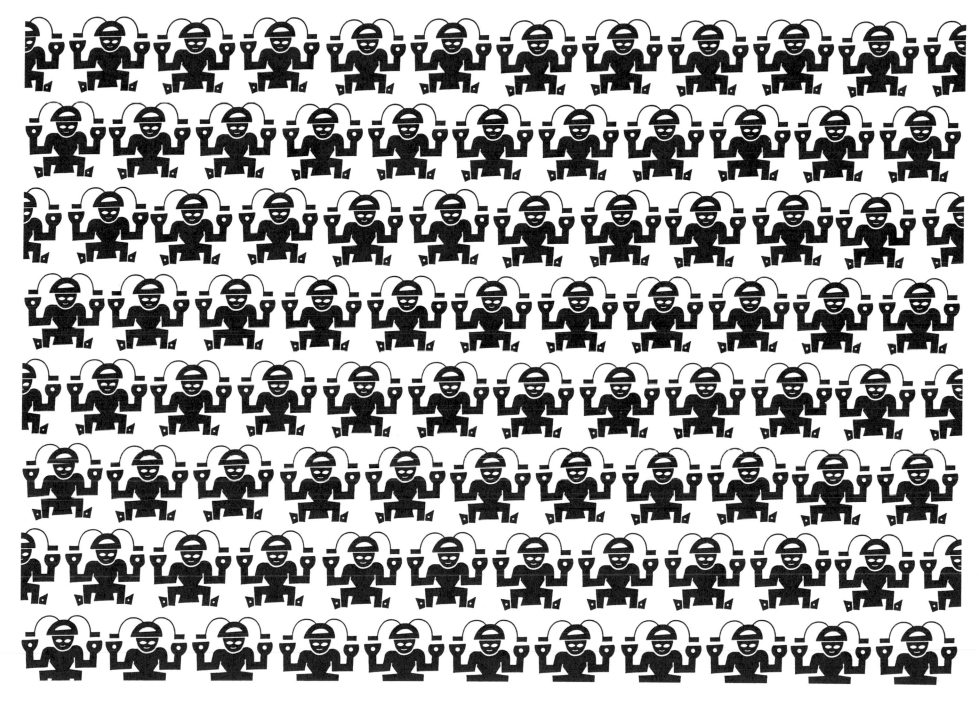

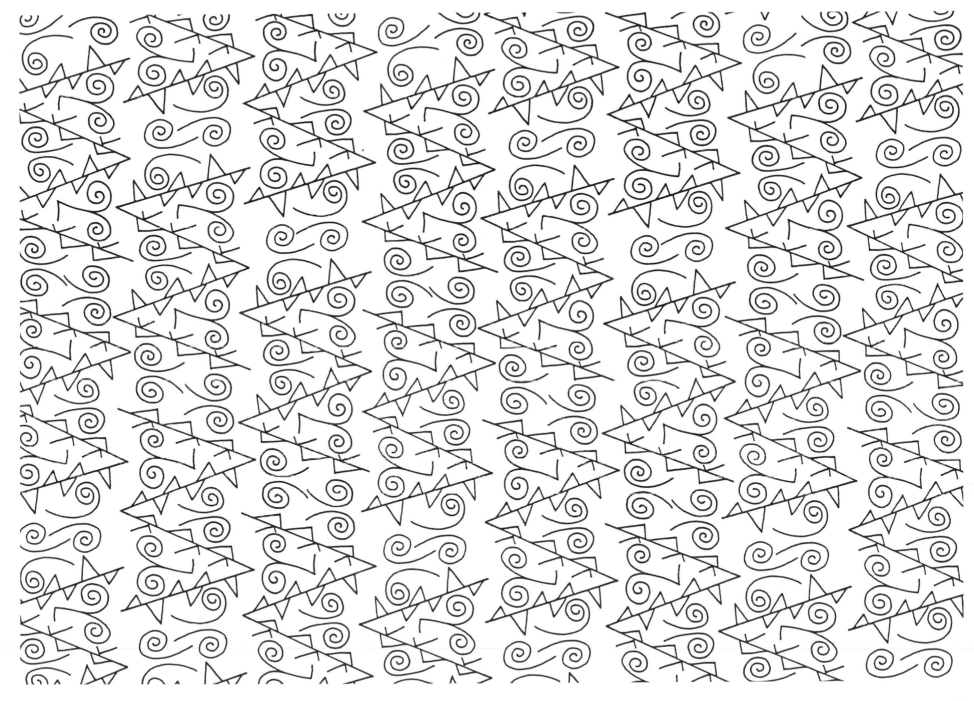

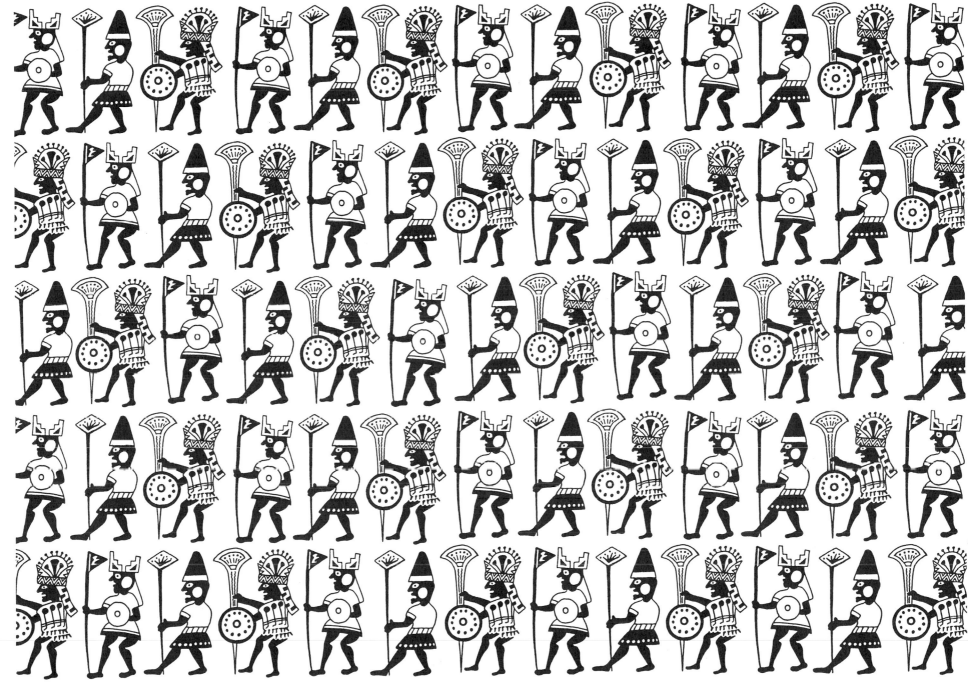

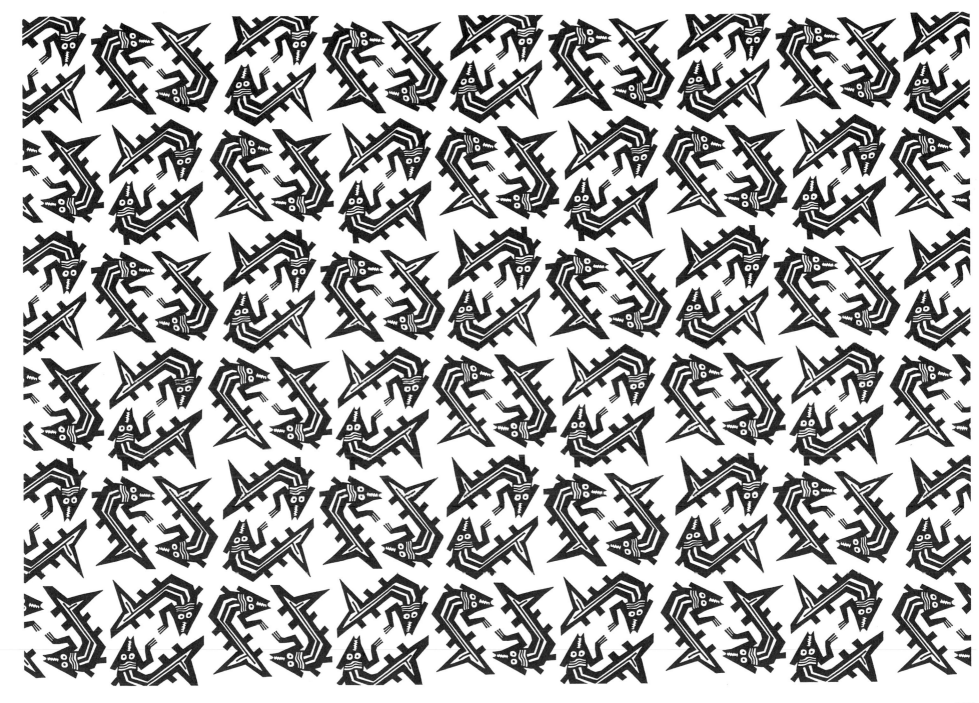

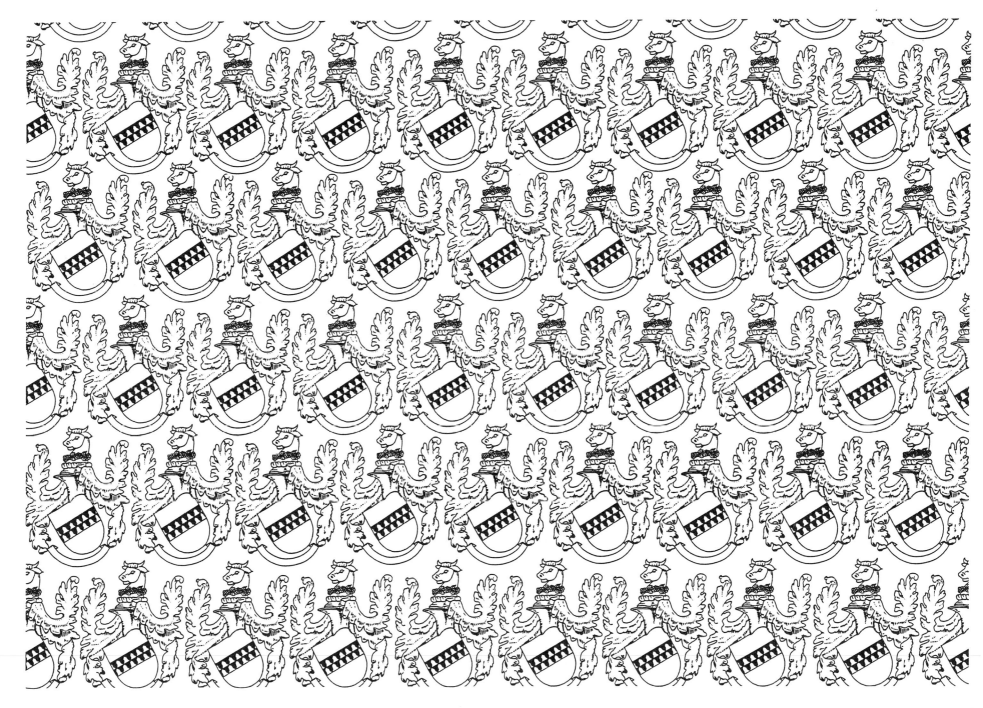

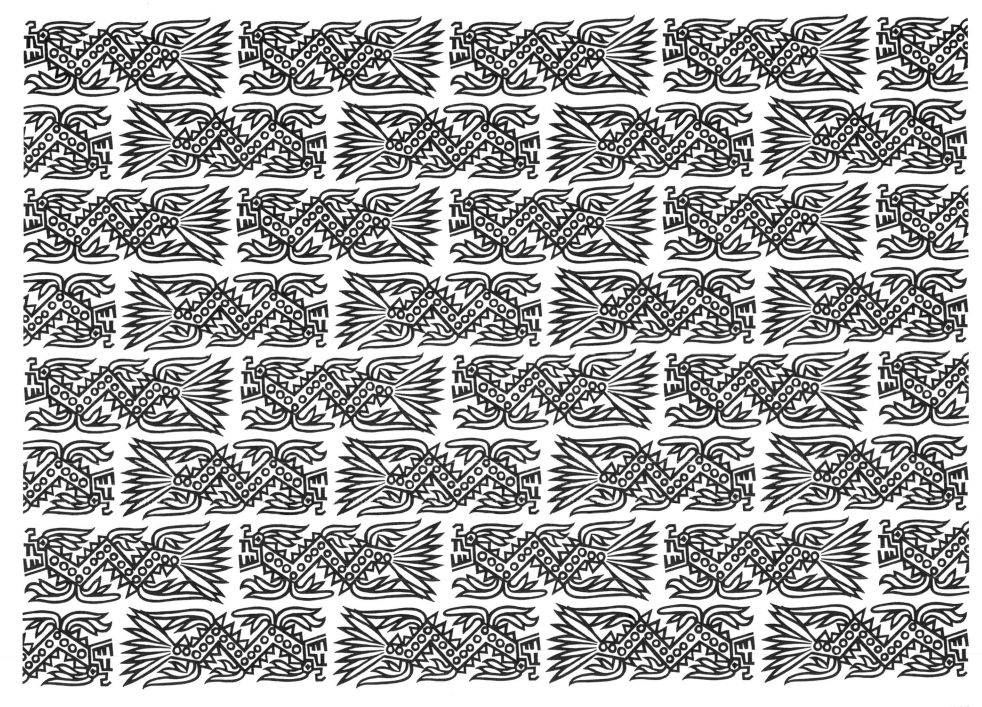

NOTES

NOTES